Praise for

WHEN THE WORLD BREAKS

"Jason's words are the antidote we need right now, a mean-
ingful offering beyond cynicism and apathy...An absolutely
beautiful book."

—Shauna Niequist, *New York Times* bestselling
author of *I Guess I Haven't Learned that Yet*

"I deeply loved this book. Not only is Jason Miller one of my
favorite pastors I've ever known, but now I have to add him to
my list of favorite authors. An important book for our current
cultural conversation."

—Scott Erickson, author of
Honest Advent and *Say Yes*

"For a long time, words of Jesus have seemed to be held
hostage by people determined to make them complicated and
confusing. What this book does is make those words simple
and beautiful and hopeful again. This book is absolutely necessary for anyone who is tired of an overly complicated Jesus
and ready for a little hope."

—Brit Barron, author of *Worth It*

"Jason Miller doesn't offer false hope that life will always be the way you want, but instead he offers a dependable hope that all will one day need. The hope that something happens on the other side of everything falling apart. With the heart of a poet and the mind of a scholar, Jason has given the world a much needed gift in writing *When the World Breaks*."

—Luke Norsworthy, pastor and author of
Befriending Your Monsters

"When your world cracks, fractures, breaks, and you feel at the end of your rope searching for any semblance of hope, trusted voices like Jason Miller are a rare gift for how they can thoughtfully guide you through the profound mystery that is your life and the ancient beatitudes. The writing and ideas are absolutely stunning and will help you discover how to kindly move forward. I didn't know how much my heart needed this book!"

—Steve Carter, author of
The Thing Beneath the Thing

"Jason has written a must-read for anyone who feels like their world is breaking—which is all of us at one point or another. If you long for a humble, nuanced perspective on suffering and hope, this book is for you. If you want to become the kind of person who helps put the world back together, there is no better person to learn from than Jason . . . who points us to Jesus in the most accessible and refreshing way."

—Manda Carpenter, author of
Soul Care to Save Your Life

"This is a beautiful book. It's a work that brings a defiant yet tender challenge to the loud societal voices of polarization and indifference. Jason's words rhyme with the ancient wisdom of the first Christians and the way they chose to walk. This Jesus-way is most clearly seen in the Sermon on the Mount and more specifically in the Beatitudes. I have stood many times on the Mount of Beatitudes and reflected on these words. I have never heard these ancient blessings more resonantly unpacked than in this book.

"Jason Miller is a friend who has emptied his soul onto the lines of these pages. In doing so he unveils a beautiful Jesus-looking God. I live in Northern Ireland. We have become experts in binary thinking and in the separating of 'them' from 'us.' Jason unpacks the beauty of borderland spaces. Where Jason goes, unique beauty emerges. He doesn't live in a world of false equivalence, of keeping the peace by avoiding conflict. Rather this book is an embodiment of his life, which is about setting up a tent in the borderlands, a brave space for sacred stories, where oppositional forces can find common ground and a unique forest of biodiversity can be planted and enjoyed."

—Jonny Clark, public theology program manager at the Corrymeela Community and podcaster at *Guardians of the Flame*

WHEN
THE
WORLD
BREAKS

The Surprising Hope and
Subversive Promises in the
Teachings of Jesus

JASON ADAM MILLER

NEW YORK   NASHVILLE

Faith Words
Hachette Book Group
1290 Avenue of the Americas, New York, NY 10104
faithwords.com
twitter.com/faithwords

First Edition: August 2023

Faith Words is a division of Hachette Book Group, Inc. The Faith Words name and
logo are trademarks of Hachette Book Group, Inc.

The publisher is not responsible for websites (or their content)
that are not owned by the publisher.

The Hachette Speakers Bureau provides a wide range of authors for
speaking events. To find out more, go to hachettespeakersbureau.com
or email HachetteSpeakers@hbgusa.com.

FaithWords books may be purchased in bulk for business, educational,
or promotional use. For information, please contact your local
bookseller or the Hachette Book Group Special Markets Department at
special.markets@hbgusa.com.

Unless otherwise noted, all Scripture quotations are taken from the Holy Bible,
New International Version®, NIV®. Copyright © 1973, 1978, 1984, 2011 by
Biblica, Inc.™ Used by permission of Zondervan. All rights reserved worldwide.
www.zondervan.com. The "NIV" and "New International Version" are trademarks
registered in the United States Patent and Trademark Office by Biblica, Inc.™

Library of Congress Cataloging-in-Publication Data has been applied for.

ISBN: 9781546003502 (hardcover), 9781546003526 (ebook)

Printed in the United States of America

LSC-C

Printing 1, 2023

For Alex

Now when Jesus saw the crowds, he went up on a mountainside and sat down. His disciples came to him, and he began to teach them.
He said:
"Blessed are the poor in spirit,
    for theirs is the kingdom of heaven.
Blessed are those who mourn,
    for they will be comforted.
Blessed are the meek,
    for they will inherit the earth.
Blessed are those who hunger and thirst for righteousness,
    for they will be filled.
Blessed are the merciful,
    for they will be shown mercy.
Blessed are the pure in heart,
    for they will see God.
Blessed are the peacemakers,
    for they will be called children of God.
Blessed are those who are persecuted because of righteousness,
    for theirs is the kingdom of heaven."

Matthew 5:1–10

CONTENTS

FOREWORD

During the summer of 2020, when we all came to the edge of ourselves, when the brokenness of the world seemed beyond repair and none of us knew how long we could bear the split, I was going through a personal crisis of my own. It wasn't anything you could see from the outside, but it was real and true and terrifying, as all breaking tends to be.

For months I stood at the edge of what seemed to be two pathways: Follow one and I would break all the way apart; follow the other and I would break all the way open. The question wasn't whether or not there would be a breaking, rather the question was what impact would this breaking have? These paths would lead to different outcomes, but I didn't know many pioneers to point the way. Many of the voices I had turned to in the past for direction and discernment sounded foreign to me at the time and I was desperate to find resonant voices I could stand to listen to, people who weren't afraid of mystery, who didn't spout certainties in all directions, who were well acquainted with grief.

That's when I found Jason Adam Miller, a young pastor from northern Indiana, donning all-black T-shirts and with kind eyes, with a willingness and capacity to hold paradox. In his voice and teaching, I discerned a wisdom beyond what his years would suggest. He spoke about the certainty of Jesus in a way that still left room for uncertainty of other things. He welcomed the strange mystery of our faith with a hard-won ease, and it was this open-hearted posture that drew me in.

The strangeness of some aspects of the Christian faith used to intimidate me: the passages that didn't make any sense, the culture that wasn't my own, the nuance in the sacred text of the Hebrew, Greek, and Aramaic. But when you encounter pain, when you bear witness to those who are marginalized, when you are marginalized yourself, a strange faith becomes the only kind that makes sense. Now I'm drawn to the voices singing harmony with strangeness, with this peculiar Messiah who showed up small, who grew up without great privilege, who blessed all the seemingly unblessable conditions.

When it comes to those things in life and in the world that we don't understand, author and activist Parker Palmer invites us to hold the tension longer, to refuse to jump to conclusions just to find resolution, but to be willing to sit with the questions even if they bring more questions. When confronted with the pain in the world, Palmer submits that our hearts can either break apart into a million pieces, or they can break open, making room for more. Jason is a writer who doesn't shy away from holding this tension, but grabs both ends of the rope with a relentless commitment to hope and honesty. As a result, he writes from a deep well, a heart that has been broken all the way open and makes room for more.

This is a book about what can happen when things break, about what happens when we face great loss and how we decide what to do with it. Be ready, there's no easing into this story. But I believe a few things about us that give me hope for our collective willingness to hold the tension longer, too: I believe we are aware of our deep need more than ever before, we are committed to our own healing and the healing of those around us, and we will not suffer fools. We're ready to listen to voices who fight for mercy without sacrificing justice. Jason Adam Miller is one such voice.

Here is a leader who refuses to accept a flat or sentimental interpretation of the words of Jesus. Here is a writer who is doing the hard, holy, human work of naming the nearly unnameable and bringing us along. Here is a story that begins on the northwestern shore of the Sea of Galilee, and continues to be told in us, upon the sacred ground of the inner landscape of our own lives. Lean in.

Emily P. Freeman
Author of *The Next Right Thing*

1

THE BLISSFUL EXISTENCE
OF THE GODS?

The world is breaking.

We're still recovering from a pandemic that has taken millions of lives.

Our politics are seething with division.

Forests are burning and climate change is only beginning to show us all the harm it will do.

The racial injustice that some of us were taught to think of as a matter of history while others lived with it every day is being broadcast in real time.

A fault line has cracked open. Whether it's at the hands of human agents or in the wake of some natural event, you can feel the ground shifting beneath your feet.

The breaking may not be in the headlines, though. It might be just for you. You get a call from the doctor and the diagnosis isn't good. Or you find out your vows meant something different for you than they did for your spouse. Or maybe you feel the world breaking when your long-held beliefs about God or the Bible or faith slowly or suddenly slip through your fingers and the thing that acted as your compass is no longer there.

Whether the details are global or personal, the experience is the same: You discover that the framing reality you were living in has fractured. You experience this framing reality in the way your relationship with your parents and your job and the color of your skin and your beliefs about God and the investment return on your 401(k) and the latest update from the war on terror all conspire to tell you that you exist and that you're a part of some coherent order in the world. To tell you that you're going to be okay. But what happens when that changes?

This isn't just a book about bad things happening. It's about what happens when the fundamental picture we had relied on—our sense of how everything holds together—falls apart. This is what we sometimes mean by the word *suffering*, and if we don't do something with our suffering, other forces will.

When the world breaks, bad religion will seize the moment. If the preachers can shame you, convincing you that a more faithful person wouldn't be suffering like this, they'll have all the power they need. They may sell you indulgences or demand your allegiance. If it isn't shame that bad religion invokes when the world breaks, it may be escapism instead. Fantasies of a future where we can leave this mess behind are especially enticing when everything falls apart.

If it's not bad religion that takes advantage of the moment, it may be addictive substances that fill the void instead. If we can just find a way to stay numb, we may not have to feel the pain of the breaking. It's a ruse, of course. Those addictions create all new kinds of pain.

When the world breaks on the level of war or economics or terrorism or a pandemic, demagogues in the political sphere will inevitably seize the opportunity to divide and conquer us.

They'll weaponize our fear and teach us to become enemies. A quick survey of world history shows that some of the most violent leaders found their way to power in moments when the populace was feeling the ground quaking beneath their feet. Everyone wants a benevolent authoritarian when they feel unsafe. When suffering is at hand, it can be exploited for the worst kinds of things.

But here's the good news:

The world has been breaking for as long as we can remember.

I know—that may not sound like good news.

But it is, because it means we've been here before. And if we've been here before, then we can turn to ancient, perennial wisdom to help us sort through these urgent problems. And if we turn to that ancient wisdom, we may discover some surprises.

There are hidden possibilities lurking in these moments. They're not revealed in some quaint moral teaching. They're not found in the "power" of optimism that turns out to be nothing more than denial wrapped in an exhausting attempt to generate positive energy from scratch. They have nothing to do with the power to hit back, to break more things in response.

These possibilities are expressed in the subversive promises Jesus spoke when he taught the eight blessings—often called the Beatitudes—recorded in the beginning of Matthew chapter 5. These strange blessings name our experiences of suffering and are built on a surprising vision of hope. This book is a meditation on those teachings as a transformative way forward when we suffer.

———

To understand the strangeness of these blessings, it helps to have some background on the language of Matthew 5.

The ancient Greeks imagined that their gods experienced the best kind of life. They were up there in the clouds, or high atop Mt. Olympus, and the frail, fraught world down here, with all its chaos and violence, was far from them. The Greeks had a word for this experience: They called it *makarios*, and according to one philosopher,* it meant the blissful existence of the gods. This word *makarios* shows up in Greek texts that have been translated into English, and often in those translations, this word is rendered *blessed*.

Around the same time that the Greeks were thinking about the blissful existence of the gods, the Jews were imagining a different kind of blissful existence. It was available to human beings who lived virtuously, because people who lived virtuously could depend on the protection of God as a reward. They imagined a kind of insurance policy against suffering, and the

———

* I got this from a book by Dallas Willard called *The Divine Conspiracy*. If you haven't read it, please stop reading my book and go read his. Seriously—it may not be a best seller, but I can't tell you how much it has influenced me and a lot of others. Willard is one of those quiet, humble elders whose work went on to shape a lot of the people who have had very public, admired careers. And also, like I said, people like me.

word for that protected status was *ashrei*. It, too, shows up in texts that have been frequently translated into English, and often this word is rendered... you guessed it: *blessed*.*

So when the gospel of Matthew is written in Greek telling the story of a Jewish man who spoke Aramaic, and we read there in chapter five that the first word of Jesus' teaching is *blessed*, we can gather up the ancient sentiments around this idea and feel the expansive promise of this opening word. Jesus is going to tell us about our path to the blissful existence of the gods. He's going to tell us about the kind of life that enjoys a divine insurance policy against suffering.

But there's a problem. If *blessed* describes this invincible kind of life, then the rest of what Jesus says makes no sense. With his first word, he tells the crowd that he will be describing the kind of person who has access to the blissful, suffering-free life, but then he goes on to describe people who are going through the absolute worst.

He says those who have a poverty within them are blessed.

He says those who have been shattered by loss are blessed.

He says those who have no power to attain for themselves the things they need are blessed.

He says those who ache for things to be made right within them or around them are blessed.

This doesn't sound like the blissful existence of the gods. It's clearly not a description of people who have enjoyed some

---

* Psalm 1, for example.

kind of divine insurance policy against suffering. He's naming the most painful human experiences. He's talking about what we feel when the world breaks, and when it breaks us, and he sounds pathologically ungrounded.

Anyone who teaches these blessings or beatitudes as a nice, logical, tidy set of instructions for good Christians isn't paying attention. Jesus is either totally naïve or he's doing something unexpected, something way deeper than a simple, straightforward prescription for pious people.

———

A few years ago, I found myself having to defend the idea that Jesus wasn't naïve. I was in Washington, DC, having dinner with a couple of people who are working to transform the conflict between Israelis and Palestinians toward a more just and peaceful arrangement. One of them, a new acquaintance for me that night, was a human rights lawyer who advocates for one of the factions in the conflict. The other, an old friend, asked me to share something I had been telling him earlier, about a way that I thought one of Jesus' teachings could be a resource for people working on this problem. But let me back up a bit.

My first trip to the Middle East was in 2010. I went there to learn about the conflict between Israelis and Palestinians. I think I expected an academic encounter, but what I experienced was a crucible of empathy and impossibility. Our little group of five pastors from the States sat with an Israeli mother whose son had been shot and killed by a Palestinian sniper in cold blood. Later that same day we shared a meal with a Palestinian father whose twelve-year-old daughter had been shot and killed by Israeli soldiers when they mistook his car for that of a terrorist. On another day we toured an Israeli town near the Gaza strip where every playground has a bomb shelter and the residents have fifteen seconds when the sirens sound to get underground before Hamas' rockets land. Shortly after that we were in a refugee camp watching surveillance camera footage of a playground full of Palestinian children being blanketed with Israeli Defense Force tear gas canisters as the children fled.

After a few days of these encounters, I had come to the end of myself. The end of my faith. The end of my hope. The day-to-day suffering in this conflict was more than I could bear, and I wasn't even living through it. I was just sitting next to it, sitting next to its victims as they shared their stories. I was falling into despair. I kept ruminating on this dark mantra in my mind: There's no way this gets better. There's no way...

At about that point in the trip, we visited a little church in the West Bank where a highly regarded elder named Abuna Elias Chacour is the priest. Chacour has been nominated for the Nobel Peace Prize. He's a legend in this part of the world.

The steps that lead you up the hillside into his church are engraved with the Beatitudes, those strange blessings that Jesus taught at the beginning of his sermon in Matthew 5. I walked right over them without much notice.

As I entered the church, I noticed icons—devotional images

of saints—everywhere. There was a brown-skinned man portrayed in an icon near the back of the church, and I felt drawn to him, so I asked someone from the church who the saint was.

"Jesus," he said.

Oh.

(I was used to Swedish Jesus with blond hair and a blue sash to match those steely blue eyes.)

Jesus was holding a book in his hands with a page open for us to read, but the text was in Arabic, so I asked what it said.

"'I am the way, the truth, and the life.'"

Oh.

That's something Jesus says in the gospel of John, in the New Testament. These are words that the Christians I grew up with cared about a lot, so I had heard them many times. But whenever I heard Christians talking about them, they didn't really mean anything for the world I lived in every day. I had been taught that they were about another time when some of us would get to leave this broken world behind.

But I had been ruminating on that dark mantra—there's no way this gets better—and my despair was growing, so I was desperate and open and for the first time in my life I heard those words in a whole new way. What I heard from that brown-skinned icon was: "There is a way that things get better, and that's what I've been trying to show you."

I went back to my hotel room that night and opened my Bible. This was the same Bible that I had used for years for personal reading and prayer, for study and preaching. Most of its pages were marked up from all that work. But the page in Matthew 5 with those blessings was pristine. Untouched. Those verses hadn't really mattered to me until then.

I felt myself pulled toward these strange blessings, as if there were something urgent and true in them that had nothing to do with the trite preaching I had heard about them in the past. In fact, I suspected that the strangeness of what Jesus was saying was a clue to its meaning. And the more I learned from the people who are doing the bravest, most beautiful work in the most broken places to put things back together, the more convinced I became that Jesus was onto something.

So a few years later when I found myself in DC having dinner with those two people talking about conflict, my friend asked me to share something from the reflecting I had been doing. When you're a pastor and someone asks you to talk about Jesus, even if you're not sure it's the right timing, it's pretty hard to say no. But before I could respond, the human rights lawyer cut me off.

"No offense," she said, "but Jesus has nothing to do with this. We're talking about a deeply entrenched conflict in which people are oppressed by a very complicated status quo involving politics and militaries and ethnic and religious biases and foreign interests who are using the land and people in question as a proxy for their own geopolitical power games..." And the more she described the context, and how it had nothing to do with Jesus, the more I was reminded of how similar it was to the context in which Jesus lived. The Jewish people in the first century had suffered exile and occupation for centuries. Their homeland was constantly being claimed by different empires that wanted it to serve their trade routes. Their religion was seen as suspect by the cults of their day. If Jesus had been naïve or simplistic, dropping cheap platitudes from a privileged place, his message wouldn't have found any traction with people who lived every day with a world that was breaking. The things he said and did were disruptive to the disorder that he and his people inhabited, and if they hadn't been, I don't think we would have even heard of him today.

———

So I want to turn to those blessings that Jesus speaks, because they point us to the promise and possibility hidden within every breaking moment. I don't believe they're moral lessons about how to be the kind of person God wants to bless. I don't think they're descriptions of what a good Christian should be like. In fact, I don't think they're specifically for Christians at all. I think they're for humans. I have come to understand them as paradoxes we cannot solve but that we can dance with, and that if we trust them, we'll discover a way forward when the world breaks. And we are desperate for a way forward.

The last decade of my life has brought me face-to-face with too many breaking points. The journey has taken me around the world, to sit with Israelis and Palestinians and hear their stories of hurt and hatred and creativity and peacemaking;

to the Beqaa Valley of Lebanon to enter the tents of Syrian refugees and sip tea with them while they tell me of the barrel bombs dropped on their homes, striking terror in their children and forcing them to flee; to Northern Ireland, where so much healing is still needed in response to the sectarian violence of The Troubles while Brexit threatens to disrupt the current peace; to Sri Lanka and Kenya to work with young leaders from around the world who have seen more terror and violence in their neighborhoods than I've seen in my life, but who somehow live with more bravery than I've ever known.

I pastor a church in the heart of a city where the fault lines of racial and economic inequality that are shaping our national discourse are local matters. I've sat in mental health facilities with members of our church as they heal from their suicide attempts. Like most pastors, I've walked with our people through unexpected loss in every form.

I've watched someone I love nearly destroyed by addiction, a front row seat in a cruel theater, seeing them teeter on a precipice that I was powerless to rescue them from.

I've walked through the collapse of my own mental health when memories of childhood trauma surfaced, triggering a five-year depression that culminated in a ten-day psych ward stay of my own.

It's through these experiences—from the global and political to the private and personal—that I've begun to recognize the terrain of reality that Jesus describes in the Beatitudes. There are reliable patterns that emerge in suffering.

Often, the ways we react to a breaking world end up breaking us or breaking the world further. We return violence with
violence, against ourselves or others. We let fear bring out the
worst in us, and we give our world over to leaders who manip-
ulate that fear for the sake of their power. We stop trusting
others because someone wasn't trustworthy once. We hold on
to the negative energy that the breaking created, and then are
surprised to discover that it begins to break us. We become
instruments of violence precisely by trying to protect ourselves
from it.

Or, as one cultural anthropologist put it: "Men cause evil by
wanting heroically to triumph over it."*

But it doesn't have to be that way.

In the paradoxes of Matthew 5, Jesus begins by helping
us abide our powerlessness. He knows that healing is usually
located in the places we most want to avoid. He knows that
we can actually embrace our emptiness and face our pain. As
we do so, we relinquish the kind of counterfeit power that we
grasp for when we suffer, leaving open the possibility that we
could get our hands on the real thing.

And then, in the final Beatitude, Jesus blesses those who
are persecuted because of righteousness or justice. I don't
think he's talking about American Christians whose egos are
stinging from being told "Happy holidays" instead of "Merry
Christmas." This is a blessing for heroes. A blessing for people

* Earnest Becker, *Escape from Evil.*

14

so powerful, so potent, that evil has marshaled its limited resources to target them.

It's as if he assumes that the same sad, powerless victims he's speaking to at the beginning could become such a threat to the disorder that evil will have to come after them.

As if in suffering, we can cooperate with a mystery that will lead us into real power.

As if we can become the kind of people who put things back together.

This is how I've come to understand hope. It arrives when we realize that nothing taken from us can defeat us. When we discover that the pain we've been running from was never going to destroy us. When we become acquainted with the healing mysteries that are laid bare in our most difficult experiences. When we discover that God is growing us up into our shared calling as healers.

———————

Before we jump in, a few things you may want to bear in mind:

First: If the word God doesn't work for you or Jesus is uninteresting to you, that's okay. I understand. This book is going to talk about God, and it's built around some of Jesus' central teachings, but for thousands of years people from all sorts of different perspectives have found some common ground in these teachings, regardless of what they believe or don't believe. I think you will, too. I'm not writing this to get you to join the club. I just want to share something that I think we could all stand to hear.

 Second: A lot of books about suffering try to explain it. They address questions like: Why are we suffering? And how could God allow this? This isn't one of those books. While brilliant people have worked out some thoughtful responses to questions like those, in my experience, most people trying to answer such questions for others end up saying stupid, harmful things. And when you're in the middle of it, I'm not sure that a metaphysical diagram of cause and effect is really what you need.

Third: Because we're talking about the subversion and surprises in these blessings, don't expect them to fit into the categories we've created to make sense of the world. They're designed to subvert them, which means this may not be a quick read. Give yourself permission to put this book down and think or meditate or pray (or throw it against a wall) as often as you feel the need.

Fourth: The only thing in this book that I'm an expert on is my own experience. In everything else I'm an amateur. A student. I'm a student of this text in Matthew 5, and I'm not pretending to have the authoritative reading on what those words mean. I can only describe what they've done in me. I'm not an expert on trauma, but I love to learn from people who are. I'm not a mental health professional, but I believe mental health is something we all need to work on together. I'm not an expert on conflict transformation or peace studies, but when I spend time with the experts, I always come away feeling like I've gotten a little closer to some of the most important truths we can know. That's why this book doesn't focus primarily on systemic change or the work of public justice, although it will include references to that work. I'd rather you turn to qualified practitioners for those lessons. This book focuses on the personal journey that helps us enter and sustain that work.

And speaking of professionals, the last thing to tell you before we begin is this: I believe in professional help and serious engagement with the best methods we have for healing today, whether the healing is personal or societal. I believe in therapists and twelve-step groups and learning from real practitioners of peace. I believe in taking your meds and showing up at treatment centers. Naming the spiritual realities in our suffering isn't some way of dismissing the physical and neurological and emotional and political and pharmacological realities. It's just that I think we should try to wrap our arms around the mysteries that are lurking in the midst of all of those other important things.

So with those disclaimers aside, let's see if we can get at those mysteries . . .

2

THE SOUL IS NOT A CLOSED SYSTEM

Blessed are the poor in spirit,
    for theirs is the kingdom of heaven.

On November 13, 2015, a band called Eagles of Death Metal was performing at the Bataclan theater in Paris when terrorists entered the venue with assault rifles and opened fire, wounding hundreds and killing ninety people. The French had recently carried out air strikes against ISIS targets and this was an act of retaliation. The news came just as I was headed out of my home to a venue in my neighborhood to see some live music. The alignment between the setting where that massacre had happened and the place where I was headed had me rattled, but I still went.

Some people feel the Spirit most easily in cathedrals. I sometimes sense a holiness deep in the woods or on a coast when waves hammer the shore. But for me, if there's one place that always feels sacred, it's a music venue—especially a small rock venue that specializes in indie bands where, if the house lights were turned up, you might be uncomfortable with the condition of the place. I don't know many things more human and beautiful than a crowded room with beats throbbing and melodies soaring and artists giving everything and crowds giving everything in return. The exchange of energy and vulnerability, the solidarity with strangers, maybe a good drink from the bar, and it feels like we're being given something we don't deserve. Because it's a setting I find so sacred, I felt the evil of an attack on a crowd in the middle of a show more viscerally than a lot of the violence we too often hear about in the news. It was hard not to imagine the horror inside the Bataclan. One of the members of Eagles of Death Metal also tours in a band with a friend of mine, and he tells me they still notice him scanning for emergency exits every time they enter a new venue.

When the show I went to that night was done, friends I was with were headed out for a drink, and I was tempted to join. I say "tempted" for a reason. With that absurd kind of violence in the headlines, I felt the draw to head out and let the night be filled, but it would have been an escapist move. At that time in my life, I was learning to trust another impulse in moments like this. I remember feeling aware that this was an opportunity to be responsive to this new understanding. Instead of filling the night, I went back to an empty house and tried to tend to the feelings that came with the news from Paris. Except I'm not sure *feeling* is the word for it. *Feeling* suggests something nameable. Something with its own content or shape. The thing I'm talking about is more like a lack of feeling.

———

Cole Arthur Riley, the creator behind the @BlackLiturgies Instagram account, wrote a piece for *The Atlantic** in response

———
* You can find her piece by searching for "You Don't Need to Post About Every Tragedy" at theatlantic.com.

to the pressure she feels to have a comment or opinion on every tragedy in "a world of so many traumas and terrors." In the piece, she described the need when these horrible things happen to tend to "the quiet, [where] we at last hear the sound of our own interior world. The pain or numbness. The guilt. The nothing at all."

The nothing at all.

That's what I'm trying to describe.

Weeping. Anger. Denial. Blame. Distraction. Addiction. These are the quick moves we make when the world breaks. But they often obscure something harder to name that we also encounter in suffering:

nothing.
emptiness.
absence.

It's often the sheer emptiness that goes unnoticed because it's hard to notice *nothing*. But we spend so much energy reacting to it, even if we haven't noticed it. We work so hard to protect ourselves from it, even if we've never named it. We have so many strategies to distract ourselves from it, even if we don't know what it is we're running from. It isn't the events of our suffering that we really want to get away from. It's the effects. And this peculiar effect—the emptiness, the nothing at all— might be the most insidious of all of them.

When Jesus begins his sermon in Matthew 5 with his

strange list of blessings, this emptiness is the first thing he names.

———

Jesus begins the Beatitudes by saying, "Blessed are the poor in spirit, for theirs is the kingdom of heaven."* Ever since this teaching was recorded, there have been debates about what he meant. Who are the poor in spirit? Are they different from simply the poor, which is who Jesus blesses in Luke's version of the same teaching? Does Luke have Jesus' words right? Did Matthew add "in spirit" to soften the clear, concrete category Jesus is talking about?

Even if we stop trying to reach behind the text and instead just stick with what Matthew reports, we still have questions. Are we talking about humility? People who willingly choose to leave behind their pride? A lot of people have thought that, especially in interpretations coming from the earliest centuries after Jesus.

Others have seen the first blessing as a call to empty one's life of the things that compete with God. Rebekah Eklund wrote a book that surveys historical interpretations of the Beatitudes, and she summarizes that view like this: "A person must empty herself before there is room for God."†

———

* Matthew 5:3.
† Rebekah Eklund, *The Beatitudes through the Ages*.

I don't know about that. I know I grew up hearing a lot about emptying ourselves, about humbling ourselves, about taking on all these postures, about effecting our own conditions so that somehow God would see that we had made ourselves ready for God. And because I so badly wanted God, I tried to contort myself into these postures and wondered why nothing ever really seemed to come of them.

A lot of us who grew up in religious spaces know the feeling that comes with this kind of teaching. It's like God is dangling a carrot in front of you—God's presence, blessing, healing, power, hope—and there's something you have to do to reach the carrot or finally deserve it.

Hang your head low enough.

Stop making so many mistakes.

Control yourself.

Lose the pride.

Think more about others.

Think less of yourself.

You try to bend yourself into whatever shape you've been told God most approves of, only to find yourself contorted with no carrot to show for it.

Sometimes this message is explicit, but I've found more often that it's subtle. It's implied in everything but never said out loud. Preachers and parents and teachers and friends are all working with this operating system even if they never recognize it themselves or name it for you. But the unnamed things aren't less powerful because they go unnamed—they're more damaging.

This is painful enough in ordinary conditions. But when we suffer, it's excruciating. If you come to these Beatitudes in the middle of a breaking moment and all you've ever heard is that these blessings are asking you to be something that you aren't right now, to perform something that you haven't accomplished yet, to ascend to a virtuous elevation where the blessing is waiting for you, it's easy to either give up or die trying. I suspect this operating system is one of the reasons I never really paid attention to the Beatitudes growing up. When you're exposed to a lot of dangling-carrot theology, you develop a sixth sense for it. If that's the only way you've ever heard the Beatitudes used, and if you've discovered through a lot of trial and error in your own life that dangling-carrot theology doesn't actually create anything good or beautiful or sustainable in us, you might be tempted to ignore these words.

But then one day, when I wasn't trying to empty myself, my spirit was robbed. I found a poverty in me that seemed impossible to bear. And years later I came to see this Beatitude as a description of that experience.

———

During my senior year of high school, I was growing discontent with a cycle that had repeated itself for years. I would spend most of my summers at a camp where everything was designed to focus on what we would have called the spiritual life. The communal disciplines we practiced at the camp, like worship and reading the Bible and talking about faith with one another, helped me feel a connection to God. If you're an outsider to this kind of thing, I know it may sound strange. But for the most part I experienced it as a place with kind, genuine, loving people helping me think about big questions, about God and meaning and virtue. People who helped me believe that God wanted me to experience an intimate connection with Him.* But beyond all the programmed stuff, I think the bigger reason I felt so connected there was the amount of time I got to spend alone in nature. There were trails that ran deep into the woods, and a small lake that was good for watching sunsets, and it's on those trails and watching those sunsets that I remember feeling close to Something larger than myself.

There's a letter in the New Testament with a prayer in it that meant a lot to me during those days. (It still does.) It's in Ephesians 3, and it's a prayer for people to be empowered through an experience of the infinite love of God. The prayer asks that those who experience this love would be filled with the fullness of God.

Filled with the fullness of God.

I'm still not entirely sure what that means. But it was working on me back then. (It still is.) And when I was at camp each summer, I found a craving place in me that wanted to feel

---

* You'll notice that a lot of the time I work hard to speak of God in a way that transcends gender, but there's something personalizing about calling God Him or Her, and I don't want to lose that. And at the time I'm describing here, this is the language I would have used.

loved, that wanted to be filled, and I realized I often did dumb things in response to that craving. I hoped that if I got really focused and dialed in, God could fill this thing in me.

Whatever fervor I felt during those summers, though, quickly faded when I would come back to school. There's no scandal here. I didn't do anything especially reckless. But I could feel something alive in me each summer at camp that would go dormant when I left, and I missed that feeling.

———

Toward the end of my senior year, a couple of friends and I went to a conference for students at a Christian college a couple hours away. It was kind of strange for us to do it like that. Everyone else was there with their youth group and pastors from their church. But we went, just the three of us. I was excited to seek out that feeling I found so easily each summer, and I was thankful to have a couple of friends to do it with.

We stayed in the dorms with sleeping bags on the floors of students' rooms. The first night, before the sessions started, I found inspiration for our time there in an unlikely place. Someone had taped a piece of paper on the inside of the door of a bathroom stall, so that anyone looking for something to focus on would be confronted with what it said. It offered a simple prayer: "God, make me need you more."

That seemed like a good prayer for me at the time. The problem I was trying to solve, or the thing I couldn't figure out, was why it was so easy for me to ignore something that I felt was so important and good. Why was it so easy for me to avoid any intentionality in my life with God when I thought it would help me stay in that feeling I enjoyed so much each summer?

Desperation is also a popular sentiment in religious cultures like the one I was in. At its best, the emphasis on it taps into something wise and true. I don't know anyone who's found a path to healing, toward being more human, who hasn't discovered some form of surrender or admission of need to be a critical part of that path. Whether it's my friends working the steps in their recovery journeys or the saints and mystics of history, the evidence shows we don't get very far without it.

At its worst, though, desperation turns into a strange kind of fetish, as if God gets some perverse pleasure out of seeing us weepy and vulnerable. Like a codependent partner who needs to be needed. And then there are the religious leaders who seem to feel that same perverse pleasure.

I didn't have all this reflective distance back there in the bathroom stall, though. All I knew was that it seemed like a pretty good prayer, and I hoped it would get me to a point where I would feel that feeling I was looking for more consistently. A kind of fullness inside that would make it easier to live a good life and do good things. A feeling of inner satisfaction that would keep me from chasing false fulfillment. But those hopes are what made what happened next even harder.

I carried that prayer around with me the next day and into the evening session, where a band was playing a show for the conference. Between songs, they shared a story about someone who had written to tell the band how their music was helping them cope with their childhood memories of abuse, and in that moment, a switch flipped inside.

A Pandora's box of traumatic childhood memories opened up within. The memories flooded my senses. Experiences I had no recollection of one second prior were now all I could see and feel. I wasn't in the room with that band and my friends anymore. I was in other places, in other moments from earlier in my life, and everything I was reliving was shame-inducing and scary.*

Eventually, a lot of feelings would come. Years later I would check myself into inpatient psychiatric care, and most of that time I spent just sobbing and shaking and dealing with the intense grief that came with those traumas. (I'll share more of that story later in the book.) But what I felt that weekend, and for days after it, isn't best described as a feeling. It was more like an absence.

Before I can go further into what happened that night, and how I understand what Jesus is describing here in his first

---

* I know I'm not giving you a lot of detail here about the memories. In the absence of detail, I hope you won't make assumptions. For example, these memories had nothing to do with my parents. I'm really thankful for the home I grew up in and what a safe place it was in the midst of these other experiences.

blessing, we need to take a second to talk about the soul. My friend Kent calls it the animating breath within us. David Brooks describes it as some piece of you that has no size, weight, color, or shape but is of infinite dignity and value, a thing that rich people don't have more of than poor people, or old people more than young. I've come to think of the soul as *the part of us that holds all the parts of us together*. It's the deep place from which we live—it's the access point for real joy and profound sadness and implausible hope and righteous anger and delirious happiness. It's the part of us that transcends body and brain and emotion but that includes all those things. It's the capacity within us for spiritual depth that expands beyond the material limits of our lives. You could say it's *a container for spirit*, except you shouldn't, for reasons I'll explain soon.

I know this can be frustrating language for the rationalists, for all of us on the days when we're pretty sure there's nothing more here beyond what meets the eye. There's a lot of superstition in human history, and religious superstitions have so often been used to justify the very actions that break the world.

But here's an observation that might help. It comes from John Polkinghorne, one of the physicists credited with the discovery of the quantum particle known as the quark who also happened to be an Anglican priest.* He says our best maps of reality, whether made by physicists or theologians, always

---

* Polkinghorne makes this point in the introduction to his book *The God of Hope and the End of the World*.

include elements that can't be directly measured or observed. The things we *can* measure and observe require us to add to our picture of reality things that make sense of everything we measure and observe. Dark matter is a good example of this. It's never been directly observed, but we can't explain everything we do observe without it. This isn't unique to the world of religion or spirituality. It's an exercise you'll find played out all over scientific literature, and our world today is shaped by technologies that were made possible by scientists and other researchers who were willing to include in their models of reality things that can't be directly observed.

I don't think you can make sense of human experience without some notion of the soul. The fragments that are held together within each of us must be held by something, and the depths that are cracked open when we suffer demand language that runs deeper than mere psychology or biology. With that in mind, let me take you back to that night at the conference.

————

The best way I can describe what happened to me at the concert that night is that my soul was pillaged. It's the place where I found an unchosen poverty. For most of us, most of the time, it's as if our souls are flying through the atmosphere, vessels full of good things, and then an explosive is set off. It rips through the fuselage and the pressurized cabin becomes a vacuum. Everything is sucked out into the atmosphere. Into the void. We're left empty. That night, the Pandora's box didn't just open—it exploded in the inner chamber of my soul, and the vacuum of space took everything, leaving me with nothing within.

The nothing at all.

The irony is that the feeling I was most looking for with God, the thing I was most hoping to get from my faith, was a feeling of fullness. Instead I found myself feeling totally, unspeakably empty.

I was unable to speak or look people in the eye for a few days. I think I was afraid that if someone could look me in the eye, they'd figure out I wasn't human anymore. Just a shell walking around with a dark, empty center.

This unchosen *nothing at all*, this undesired evacuation of the soul, is the way I've come to understand "poor in spirit."

———

I mentioned in the first chapter that these Beatitudes are absurd. If *blessed* means blissful, divine, suffering-free life, but the first situation Jesus applies it to is something like what I've just described, then he sounds confused.

I'm guessing that's why a lot of teachings on the Beatitudes bend them in artificial directions. They either become rigid moral prescriptions, as if God likes it when we go through the thing I've just described, and we should conjure up that circumstance in order to be rewarded for it. Or they become stripped of their strangeness by being reduced to a generic summary of the grace of God. But that glosses over the distinctiveness of what Jesus is saying. The trick isn't to gloss over it. You've got to lean into it.

If you set "blissful, divine, suffering-free life" next to "a soul robbed and left barren of any good thing" and try to figure out the relationship between these two ideas, you really have two options.

You either have a contradiction—these two things can't coexist.

Or you have a paradox.

A paradox is spoken when you set two things side by side that seemingly contradict, but that on a deeper level (maybe a level deeper than the one we've been living at) belong together. If you have a paradox on your hands, it may be that someone is trying to communicate something that exists at the edge of language.

One of the problems with trying to communicate deep spiritual truths is that it can be hard to describe a terrain to people who have never seen it before, or who have never heard language to describe that landscape even if they've walked it many times. It's one thing for me to describe the land here in Northern Ireland (where I'm sitting right now writing this paragraph) if you've seen places like it. If I tell you it's dark and green, with soft mountains and hard coastal edges, and you've already seen other places like that and heard those words for those kinds of things, then you're going to get the picture. But it's entirely different if you've never seen the color green or a mountain before, or if you have, but have never heard anyone call it "green" or "mountain."

There's a word in Christian tradition for the deeper things that exist at the edge of language. It's a word for something that's profoundly true but not obvious. Something that's real but that we're unlikely to see or understand unless it's revealed to us.

That word is *mystery*. It's not a mystery because it's unsolved, like a Sherlock Holmes story. And it's not that it's never been said before. A mystery is a mystery because it defies our everyday instincts. Because it comes from a higher level of existence, which is to say a deeper level of awareness, than the levels we live at most days. A mystery speaks to us from the realm of spirit when we're living in the flesh. According to the theologian Matthew Fox, speaking in paradoxes is "one way we invent to talk of mystery."*

If Jesus is speaking in paradoxes, describing mysteries, while naming the things we endure when we suffer, it suggests that these breaking moments reveal a hidden opportunity. That's what we're here to explore.

———

After Jesus gives the paradox of blessing the poor in spirit, he says they have the kingdom of heaven. This is how he justifies

---

* Matthew Fox, in his book *Meister Eckhart, A Mystic-Warrior for Our Times,* when talking about a way of knowing God that's described as apophatic, in conversation with Thich Nhat Hanh.

his absurd idea. This is the other part of the mystery. The deep truth that isn't obvious to us. But what does he mean by saying that we have the kingdom of heaven when our souls are emptied?

The kingdom of heaven is the promise Jesus makes throughout the gospel of Matthew. You could say it's the realm in which God's will is realized. Another way of saying it is that it's Ultimate Reality—when every illusion is erased, and when every temporary arrangement falls away, the kingdom of heaven is the thing that will remain. But to be even simpler, let's just say it's *the life of God.*

Throughout his life, Jesus keeps saying and demonstrating in all kinds of different ways that God wants to give God's life to us and live God's life through us. It's here in the Beatitudes. It's demonstrated in his healings. It's expressed in his parables. It's even there in the sacrament of the Eucharist, the meal he gives us where we sustain ourselves by consuming his own life. This is good news because anything that isn't God—anything that isn't a part of Ultimate Reality—isn't going to last.

Now, if God is the kind of thing that can be possessed or contained, then the best kind of vessel for the gift is one that's impermeable. You'd want to lock God up in a safe. But surely God isn't the kind of thing that can be possessed or contained. This is why, though we may be tempted to think of our souls as containers for spirit, we'd be better off to think of them as conduits. Conduits and containers may be similar, but when a container is permeable, we call that a leak. When a conduit is permeable, we call it functional.

36

The soul is not a closed system. If we're going to allow the life of God to flow through us, we may have to unlearn some of the ways that we've come to defend our souls. For us to be conduits, there has to be something permeable about us. In the center of our being, there has to be an openness. If there's nothing permeable or vulnerable about us, it will be hard for anything to flow through us.

We learn early, usually without ever naming the lesson, that we have been given vulnerable souls. This is a beautiful but terrifying feature of the human experience. And there's a fine, often blurry line between vulnerable and fragile. So over time we learn to build a hard case to protect this permeable, vulnerable thing within.

The case looks different for different people.* For some, it's an ability we develop to sense the preferences of others in the room and conform ourselves to those preferences. We figure out whatever is esteemed in this particular environment, and

---

* You may be familiar with the Enneagram, but as it grows in popularity, it's also losing its power as people misunderstand its purpose. Each type or number is a description of a case like I'm describing here, but the Enneagram was never meant to simply affirm the hard case. That coffee mug your Enneagram-loving friend got you that tells the world about your type-based preferences? It may not be helpful if it's just reinforcing the shell. The Enneagram's best use is to invite us to come back to the vulnerable thing inside that the case was built to protect. We don't have to get rid of the case. But we have to find a way to live from what's within again, which means knowing how to open the case. The first level of Enneagram awareness is the way it names and even honors our defense systems. But if we stop there, not only have we missed out on its wisdom, but we've actually used it to reinforce the very thing it's meant to help us leave behind.

then we fashion ourselves in that image. Some of us build a case out of our capacity for dominance. We develop a strength of will, a certain kind of power to assert against others as a way of making sure they don't assert any control over us. Some of us make ourselves experts in areas of knowledge so that we can flex that knowledge as a way of keeping our distance from the vulnerability of actual experience and relationship. The variations on the case go on and on, but the basic idea is the same: We build something around the soul to protect it.

The case isn't necessarily bad, but if we get overinvested in the case, if we start believing more in the case than the thing it protects, we're in trouble. If the lesson we take away from our suffering causes us to overidentify with the case rather than the thing it carries, we lose something important. But if suffering happens to dismantle the case, it offers us a gift.

This is an important moment to reiterate what I said in the first chapter: I'm not trying to explain *why* suffering happens. I'm not suggesting that finding something useful in suffering should somehow justify it. I'm not saying God has engineered these experiences. The idea that God may be able to work with the experience of our suffering—that God may have found a way to use the poverty in our souls as an opportunity to give God's own life to us—isn't an attempt to explain suffering. It's just an observation that Jesus seems to be making about the surprising possibilities of what can happen when things break, and it's been my own experience, too.

———

Thomas Merton was a Trappist monk who became known both for his spiritual writings and his advocacy related to social issues like war and racism. He wrote extensively about our life with God, and in one of his most famous works, *New Seeds of Contemplation*, he describes what contemplation is and what it isn't. He's talking about how it is that we come to be present with God's own life. This is another way of talking about receiving the kingdom of heaven.

In that book, he says that in the process of contemplation, in receiving the kingdom of heaven, a kind of purging has to happen within us. He says that "even apparently *holy* conceptions are consumed along with all the rest. It is a terrible breaking and burning of idols, a purification of the sanctuary, *so that no graven thing may occupy the place that God has commanded to be left empty*: the center, the existential altar which simply 'is.' "*

The impoverished soul is blessed because the conditions that made its impoverishment possible—its openness, its vulnerability—are the very same conditions that make it a good conduit for God's life in us, for the divine life to flow through us.

———

* Thomas Merton, *New Seeds of Contemplation*, pg. 13.

But this goes further, deeper still. What if an open soul—vulnerable to emptying but available to be filled—isn't just the way we find the life of God in us?

What if that very openness and emptiness *is* the life of God?

Not long after the life of Jesus, as people grappled with all these mysteries that had been expressed in his life, they began to develop language for what had been expressed. Some of that language shows up in a mystical hymn in the New Testament letter called Philippians. The consensus among scholars is that this was a very early song sung by Christians, and it begins "Christ, being in very nature God, did not consider equality with God something to be grasped, but made himself nothing…" That's a common English translation. But that's not quite what the original text says. In the Greek, where we read "made himself nothing," the word is *ekenosen,* which comes from the word *kenosis.* Kenosis means "empty." The hymn says that Jesus emptied himself. To flesh this out further, we could say that *it is in the very nature of God for God to empty Godself of God.*

There's the paradox again: It is in the nature of God to empty Godself of God. I know—that might make your head spin a bit. That's what it does to me. As long as it stays theoretical and theological, it can feel too heady. I'm not even sure what it means. But when I remember that night at the conference, and when I remember the emptying of spirit that happened when I read about the attack in Paris, and as I learn to notice *the nothing at all* that I so often feel when the world breaks, I'm also learning to not run from that inner experience of emptiness, but rather to sit with it. To even welcome it. Because I'm learning that it's a reminder that I am a vessel for God. That divine life is ready and willing to flow through me. And that even the emptiness may be a sign that I'm in the company of the divine. And while I may not entirely understand what that means, I know the good it has done in me.

———

In Matthew 4, right before Jesus gives these blessings in chapter 5, we read that "Jesus went throughout Galilee, teaching in their synagogues, proclaiming the good news of the kingdom, and healing every disease and sickness among the people." The good news of the kingdom brings with it healing.

I've come to look back on that moment at the concert as the inciting incident of healing in my life. It forced me to confront grief and loss. It helped me begin to come back to my own body. It was the beginning of a reconciliation process with my memories. But threaded through all those pathways of healing was a spiritual journey that led me to encounter God not just in feelings of fullness, but in emptiness, too.

I've heard there's a God-shaped hole in us. Maybe you've heard that, too. Preachers talk about it and tell us that all our problems come from trying to make other things fill the hole that only God can fill. So far, so good. I do think that's a decent description of some of our problems. But then, based on that metaphor, you might think that if we could only get God, we'd be filled and happy. If we're not careful, that just makes God another commodity alongside all the others, with the one advantage that God is the commodity that fits.

A lot of religious fervor has been generated over the millennia from people desperately trying to do whatever it takes to get their hands on the commodified God. Pray harder. Give more. Earn it. It's so tempting to think that we're just one more act of devotion away from being fixed. But that conviction can actually make us sick. Desperation turns to shame. We wonder what's so uniquely, especially wrong with us that we can't get God to come be with us. We begin to interpret the emptiness we feel—an emptiness that simply goes with the territory of living with permeable souls—as a flaw, rather than a feature of our humanity.

But what if Jesus is trying to tell us that the healing begins when we simply embrace the empty place inside? Yes, stop trying to fill it with all the other commodities. But maybe stop trying to fill it with God, too. Because maybe God is already there, in the emptiness. What if God is glorified simply in the vulnerability of our souls? What if the divine life is already with us, even when we've been robbed?

———

That night at the conference when those memories erupted in me, I hadn't yet connected these Beatitudes to the suffering I faced there. But once I had that experience in the West Bank at Abuna Chacour's church, I started noticing that the terrain Jesus describes in the Beatitudes is familiar, if not obvious. It's the landscape I walked in the wake of those memories.

So that night when I heard about the attack in Paris, I went home and tried to attend to the emptiness. The nothingness. Not to wallow in it or identify with it. But to be present with it, and to observe my panicky desire to overcome it or ignore it or disconnect from it. To invest myself in my growing conviction that God is not an elusive object that I have to attain so that I can be filled. I am slowly learning what the mystics have taught us as they reflect on texts like Philippians 2 and their own experience—sometimes the fullness of the Divine life is found in the empty place inside. My brain doesn't really like that, because the math doesn't add up. But I'm learning to trust the deeper experience of the soul, where the math doesn't matter, but there are other ways of knowing that God is here. And if I have found something of God, even in the empty place, then healing is close at hand, both for me and for the world around me.

3

THE GLORY IS NOT DIMINISHED

Blessed are those who mourn,
for they will be comforted.

The 9/11 Memorial in New York City has two massive square waterfalls carved into the ground where the Twin Towers once stood. They're big enough to make you feel unsettled when you stand at their edges. The designer calls them the "voids" and says they were built to "render absence visible," because there used to be two towers there, but of course they're gone now, along with the lives of three thousand people who died in the attack.

I bring this up because whether your world breaks or the world breaks—whether it's personal or global or somewhere in between—we usually end up losing something, and when we face great loss, we have to decide what we'll do with it.

The loss may be an actual life, whether taken by violence or natural processes or someone's self-destructive choices.

Or maybe you lost a feeling of safety that you took for granted until you were robbed of it.

Many of us in the US have had to let go of a picture of our country that turns out to be naïve. America is a more complicated, unjust place than we realized. (I know—for some of you reading this right now, this isn't new information.)

You may have had a dream for the future that disappeared when the world broke, and now you're left with a gaping hole in your vision of what's to come.

It may be the loss of a relationship, and in losing that person you feel like you've lost some irretrievable part of yourself.

The loss may occur in the violation of the sacred boundaries of your life—your body, your home, your story. These boundaries surround such holy possessions that it's easy to take them for granted, because of course there's a boundary around the sacred thing we call You. When those boundaries have been violated, you may have a hard time feeling at home in your own life, and that means you've lost something. It's not that it can't be restored, but something was lost.

Almost every week I meet with people who are grappling with the peculiar grief that comes with the loss of faith. If you spent most of your life with a certain picture of God, or Ultimate Reality, or a sacred text, the dissolution of that picture can be traumatic. Maybe the suffering you've faced seemed so incompatible with your picture of God that you had to give up on it. Or maybe an intellectual journey led you to a new view of God or faith, and letting go of the old one is the suffering you're facing right now. The loss of faith can happen when we suffer, and the loss of faith can be the thing we suffer. Even if you've moved into greater truth or left behind something that didn't hold up, that doesn't mean there isn't some loss associated with that evolution. After all, for life to evolve, some things must die.

Whatever we lose when the world breaks, the loss can have a substance of its own, and we have some choices to make about what we're going to do with it. That's why I mention the 9/11 Memorial.

A lot of things could have been done with that place where the towers fell. We could have paved over and redeveloped it so you would walk there and forget what happened. We could have built new buildings on the footprint of the old ones, as if to say to our enemies, "We're stronger than what you did to us." We could have done this to send a message to our enemies, but I also suspect it would have been our way of saying something to ourselves.

The modern consciousness resists grief, and often our response to loss is really a strategy for avoiding it. Mourning can feel self-indulgent or unproductive. Or worse, it confronts us with an unsettling powerlessness.

What does it mean that we're so susceptible to violence? Are we really so vulnerable? We rush to move on from these questions because they leave us feeling impotent, shaking us to the core. These are existential questions, the kind that cut through everything and interrogate our very being. So naturally we'd like to resolve them quickly, and in comforting ways.

But that's not what we did in New York. Instead of building fresh monuments to our own power, we first built the voids. We created something to name and honor the absence. We memorialized the loss. This was an act of public wisdom. And when Jesus says, "Blessed are those who mourn, for they will be comforted," he's speaking from a tradition of wisdom that would affirm this.

———

The Bible's prayer book is called the Psalms. These prayers come from Israel's history, and they shaped and reflect the collective spirituality of those people. Before they were ever carried around in personal Bibles, they were recognized as the sacred cries of the communal heart. A thousand years after they were written and compiled, a north African bishop* described them as a mirror showing us every part of ourselves. Centuries after that, a lawyer in Geneva† discovered in the Psalms an "anatomy of the soul." These ancient prayers express a deep knowledge of our inner world and the energies that drive and shape us.

When scholars approach the book of Psalms, they generally see three kinds of prayers.‡ There are psalms of praise. These are prayers that celebrate the ordering of reality, where the pieces fit together and we know our place in everything and all is well. They often say something like, "God, you're great!" but they don't just reflect some religious experience of God. They reflect the feeling we have when the world seems whole.

Then there are psalms of thanksgiving. These are prayers that come after the world breaks and gets put back together, when you're freshly aware that things haven't always been this good and you're grateful for the healing that's happened. It's the feeling of finding your feet on solid ground after an earthquake.

And then there are prayers written when the world breaks—

---

* Saint Augustine, the fourth-century Bishop of Hippo.

† John Calvin.

‡ This way of categorizing the psalms was originally developed by a German scholar named Hermann Gunkel.

the psalms of lament. These are the ones that cry. That weep. That mourn. That protest. They accuse God of being absent. They beg God to deliver. They bleed.

If you study this book of prayers, a couple of things stand out.

First: If you take all the psalms that qualify as praise and add them up, and all the psalms that qualify as thanksgiving and add them up, and all the psalms that qualify as lament and add them up, guess which category is the biggest?

Lament.

These writers cry out for deliverance and beg for justice. Over and over again they name the voids that are created when the world breaks. Their prayers sound like this:

> *You crushed us and made us a haunt for jackals;*
> *you covered us over with deep darkness.**

Or this:

> *You have shaken the land and torn it open;*
> *mend its fractures, for it is quaking.*
> *You have shown your people desperate times;†*

Or this:

---

* Psalm 44:19.
† Psalm 60:2–3a.

51

We are given no signs from God;
no prophets are left,
and none of us knows how long this will be.*

If you were overheard offering one of these protest prayers, a well-intentioned person might chastise you for your lack of faith and encourage you to keep your head up. We're not comfortable with naked lament. In fact, some of our communities actively resist it. There are families that can't handle this. Circles of friends that reject this. Churches that run away from this. The prayers that are least welcome in some of our spiritual communities are most prevalent in this sacred text.

This tendency to run from lament isn't just inconsistent for any person or community trying to take the Bible or Jesus seriously. It's also a tragic way of cutting ourselves off from the very paradoxes that can heal us. And one of the signs of the power of lament is hidden within these psalms, which brings us to the other thing you might notice if you study them.

These prayers tend to follow a pattern: First, they name the loss, either poetically or directly, and express the pain and anger that has come from the loss.

And then they turn to praise.

Praise.

The psalm that begins, "My God, my God, why have you forsaken me?" goes on to say, "I will declare your name to my

_____
* Psalm 74:9.

52

people; in the assembly I will praise you . . . from you comes the theme of my praise."*

When I first began studying these prayers, this feature annoyed me. It felt pious, like the writers knew what the right answer was to all these questions and they had to land there whether they believed it or not. Like the counterfeit, escapist, sentimental, greeting card kind of faux spirituality that sounds good until you actually try to live inside the experience it's describing, only to find out it doesn't work. Like the naïveté that leads people to say awful things to you when you're hurting, things that are meant to be encouraging but that really just trivialize the fact that you've been shattered by what happened. I've known people who can make this quick turn from protest to praise authentically, but I've known more who have simply been told it's the right thing to do and so they make the turn while they leave their own heart behind.

However, one principle for reading sacred texts is to remember they often express in microcosm things that are bigger and take longer than is suggested on the page. If you approach these prayers knowing that, you might ask: What is it about lament that leads to praise? Is this a snapshot of a longer process? Is there some inherent connection between grieving and glory? And if so, is that what Jesus has in mind when he blesses the mourners and says they will be comforted?

---

* Psalm 22.

———

Let me tell you about my friend Alex.

He and I met in college and became fast friends. I bought a shabby old house while we were students and he moved in with me and a few other guys. We spent the next three years living together, sitting on the roof smoking convenience store cigars, going downtown to an Irish pub on Monday nights to catch up on the beer consumption that we had missed out on while attending a Christian college with rules about that sort of thing. I discovered a friend who was effortlessly cool and unfailingly kind. He could meet you at any level—he was the life of the party, but he was also the guy you want to talk to when you're working out something personal or philosophical. During those years, I watched him search for a dream big and beautiful enough to channel his energies.

Eventually he found it. I came home one day and he asked me to come up to his room. On his computer he showed me what he had discovered: a fledgling nonprofit whose mission was to promote awareness and activism on behalf of the children being exploited as soldiers in Joseph Kony's war in Central Africa. I saw something light up in him, and it wasn't long before he packed up for San Diego to join them.

One of the organization's strengths was their outreach to artists who would use their platforms to spread word about the cause. Alex ended up all over the country traveling with bands, making friends everywhere he went. He would send me dispatches from tour buses and backstage greenrooms with some of my favorite rock stars. It seemed everyone fell in love with that same effortless cool and unfailing kindness.

We stayed connected through texts and phone calls and flights to see each other through the years, and he never stopped being a generous friend. One day, years after he had moved to California, an unexpected package arrived at my house. Alex had sent me a copy of Aristotle's *Nicomachean Ethics* with a page marked in the section where the philosopher discusses friendship. Aristotle said there are different kinds of friendship, and that the best kind <u>is the friendship of the good. This is the kind</u> of <u>friendship where each person is drawn</u> to the virtue of the other, <u>invested in the growth of that virtue in the other.</u> Alex had highlighted the passage describing that kind of friend and drawn a big asterisk in the margin next to it. No other note. It was a typically cool way for Alex to say something really kind.

Eventually he fell in love. Beth, the woman he would marry, ended up in Nashville, and he moved there to be with her. Then one day he started asking if I would be in Nashville on certain dates. It was Alex's roundabout way of letting me know they were planning a wedding and asking me to officiate. Soon I was standing under the canopy of a massive old tree on a Tennessee afternoon inviting Alex and Beth to make their vows to each other.

The following January, I got a text from Alex:

"Hola amigo! I thought you'd like to see the newest mini member of our family :)"

Then he sent me the ultrasound.

We celebrated together over the phone. After all his years of globetrotting, I could sense the joy he felt in digging roots, finding a home, and starting a family.

Three months later, I got a text from another friend.

"Hey dude you have a few min? Gotta tell you some news."

I called. He asked if I was alone.

Then he told me Alex had died by suicide.

When he said it, it was like the words bounced off me. I felt my mind take two steps back from reality, like I was observing a plot I wasn't a part of. There was no recognition in me to respond to what he had said. It was more than incomprehensible. It was impossible. It took a couple of days for me to feel anything, but once I began to feel, the pain was more intense than anything I have ever felt before.

I had to be in New York City that week for work, so I boarded a plane the next day still numb. But the second night of the trip, while walking the city with a couple of friends, I could feel the grief rising like nausea. I awkwardly tried to explain to my friends why I had to get away and be alone. Back in my hotel room, the sadness began to consume me. It would continue like that for months.

A couple of weeks later I went to Nashville to attend Alex's funeral and deliver a eulogy. The night before the funeral, I was settling in on the couch of a friend's house where I would be sleeping. I had a blank notebook page in front of me and needed to figure out what I would say the next day. As I stared at the blank page, one of those waves of sadness came.

I curled up into a sobbing, shaking ball, thinking to myself, I didn't know it was possible to hurt this much.

It was so much more than an emotion. It ripped through my body, as if some sliver of the violence Alex committed against himself had struck me as collateral damage. I thought of his wife, Beth, pregnant with their son, and how her grief must be orders of magnitude larger than my own. I thought of his parents. His brothers. I thought of the moments before he died, when he somehow didn't understand that there were other ways forward. I thought of how terribly alone he must have felt, even though he wasn't alone at all. I could feel my brain rebelling against the absurdity of suicide. How do you hold this much pain?

There would be a lot of people at the funeral, people who knew and loved Alex from different contexts, and I was desperate to do some justice to the moment on behalf of this unexpected congregation. But what the hell do you do with this? What do you say?

As a pastor and teacher, often my job is to help people understand things. To help them discover the coherence in something that feels unclear. But as those instincts tried to kick in, I could feel how wildly inappropriate that would be. This wasn't a moment for answers or explanations. It called for something else.

Staring at the blank page, I felt the incoherence of this kind of suffering. I prayed like I hadn't prayed in a long time, with a kind of desperation that still unnerves me as I recall it. And as I prayed and sobbed, a different kind of clarity began to grow in me. My job was simply to give witness to Alex. No answers. No explanations. I was going to build a void.

The next day I walked down the aisle of the church with Beth on one arm, the other holding the leash for their German shepherd, Kaloko, whom Alex had adored. She sat quiet and still at our feet through the service as if she knew her duty to keep vigil for Beth at that horrible event.

When it was time for me to speak, I got up and turned to face an impossible room. I'll never forget those faces. I've done plenty of funerals as a pastor. I've spoken in complicated situations. But I had never seen anything quite like that sea of anguish.

I told them stories from our years of living together in that shabby old house. About how my dog, Jack, an exuberant golden retriever, took a peculiar liking to Alex, and how he would single Alex out of any crowd for a particularly inappropriate display of canine dominance and affection.* I talked about our Monday nights at that Irish pub where we would work out some of the big questions we were chewing on, all tangled together with remnants of our adolescent angst. I told them that I could go anywhere in the world and eventually run into someone who knew and loved Alex. I told them what it was like to watch him fall in love with Beth, and how he had already become a loving father to the child she was carrying.

I told them that someone watching Alex from a distance

---

* Yes, I'm saying Jack loved to hump Alex's leg. For some reason I've never understood, more than anyone else, Jack loved to hump Alex's leg.

might have thought he was running around a lot, but that if you knew him well, you knew he had a compass in his chest with two cardinal directions—one pointing toward beauty, the other toward justice—and that all that activity and adventure were his way of working out how to follow the compass. And together we told Alex we loved him, and that we already missed him like hell.

———

The funeral continued a couple weeks later in San Diego, where Alex had moved when he left my house. The community that grew from the organization he had worked with earlier was still largely rooted there, and they wanted to honor him with a celebration. People would be flying in from around the world to be a part of this second memorial, too, but I almost didn't go.

I didn't know most of those people. And the week after Alex's funeral in Nashville, I was in Ohio on Lake Erie to scatter the ashes of my grandfather, who had died earlier that year. Combined with the loss of Alex, it left me feeling like the only thing I could do was crawl into a hole and hide for a while. A few days out, though, one of the people who was helping organize the San Diego events reached out and asked if I was coming and could say a few words. I booked my flights that night.

Alex had become a surfer during his time in California, so one of our rituals in San Diego was a paddle out. We all met at the beach on a day whose dark skies matched the mood we were in. Dozens of us grabbed surfboards and paddled out from the shore, meeting in a cluster on the ocean, holding one another in an improvised flotilla. People shared reflections and we sang together, the ocean surging and sinking beneath us as if it were channeling the same waves of grief that were pulsing through us. Then we spread out into a circle. Beth took the lei she had been wearing in Alex's honor and threw it into the middle, where it floated like an altar on the water. We dug our hands into the ocean and splashed toward the lei in an act of love and honor. We wept.

While we were out there, I thought about how I almost hadn't made the trip, and what a mistake that would have been. Something was happening out there on the water, something that had begun when I tried to find words to share at the funeral in Nashville. And while I didn't totally understand it, an instinct within told me that whatever was happening was crucial for healing, that these acts of mourning would somehow lead us into a new wholeness.

And then, that evening as the sun set over the ocean, the sky was set on fire.

I can still see and feel it as I write about it now. I say feel because it was a whole-body experience. The color and light shot through me, gripped my senses, shook my foundations. It robbed me of breath like a plunge into cold water. It was electricity in the sky. It was more than light banking off the clouds and colored by the atmosphere. It felt like the universe had been cracked open and something kept secret had been revealed. It was pleasure at the edge of my capacity to withstand it. I found myself weeping again, but not because of sadness as much as the sheer quantity of feeling, of experience, of love, of presence. It overwhelmed me, and had I not wept and shouted, I think I would have exploded.

This strange sunset was the kind of beauty that begs for other words.

Words like *glory*.

And the thing the beauty—the glory—stirred up in me was wonder.

Or rapture.

But those words aren't enough.

I think the word for it is *praise*.

This is where we come back to those psalms of lament, and a theory I have about what might be going on there.

———

The writers who gave us those ancient meditations on grief and glory inhabited the same world we inhabit, but they did so with a sacramental imagination that's hard for us to recover in this disenchanted age.* By sacramental imagination, I mean the belief that there's more than matter lurking in all the

---

* For a better understanding of this disenchantment, check out Richard Beck's book *Hunting Magic Eels*. And if you really want to dive deep, get into Charles Taylor's *A Secular Age*.

material around us. Landscapes, stories, dreams, animals, people—things were seen not just at face value, but for the glory within them. Sensing the glory in these things would move the writers to praise. They say things like:

*The heavens declare the glory of God.**

And:

You have made [humanity] a little lower than the angels, and crowned them with glory and honor.†

One of those writers uses the phrase *deep calls to deep,*‡ and I've often wondered if that's the poet's way of describing our capacity to sense the glory around us—that there is a depth within us that senses the depth around us. We are surrounded by sacraments, and despite our modern disenchantment, we still have a radar within that scans the world and recognizes them, and I think the poet is describing this inner knowing.

This capacity is what gives grief its strange power. Like a nerve ending that's exposed, our ability to sense the glory in things is what makes such profound pain possible in the loss of those things. It's why we're so tempted to turn away from

---

* Psalm 19:1.
† Psalm 8:5.
‡ Psalm 42:7.

our grief. If you've suffered, you've probably lost something. And that loss is more than a psychological inconvenience, more than the unfortunate consequence of our attachments. It is the loss of the glory that radiated in that life, that hope, that dream, that faith. And the deep within us cries out when some of that glory is taken away.

But then, because mourning reinforces this capacity within us—because in lament we turn toward it rather than ignoring it or numbing it—its sense is heightened and we may be able, if only for a moment, to sense the undiminished glory that shines in all things.

As much as we revel in the way the glory meets us in particular lives, stories, or places, our souls are also able to teach us that the glory is universal, a wholeness that cannot be diminished or fractured by loss. Not long ago, mathematicians and scientists came to understand that the total energy in a system cannot be destroyed—it simply changes forms. The mystics have been telling us this for ages. The glory is not diminished. It simply returns to its creator, and the creator keeps giving that glory back to creation. If we can live from this wholeness, we may find ourselves better equipped to put things back together in the world.

I've come to understand that sunset in San Diego as a mystical experience, but I hesitate to use that language. Most of us have gotten the impression that mystical experiences are reserved for the spiritually elite after they've climbed the holy mountain. That's not how I see it anymore. I'm talking about the kind of experience that's waiting for all of us in the dark valley if we open our hearts. It's not the only time I've had one in the wake of severe mourning. A few years prior, dear friends of mine spent six months in a neonatal intensive care unit fighting for the survival of their baby boy. I was there with them the day he was born, and I was there with them the night they were told he wouldn't make it any longer. He had spent days on a machine called ECMO that basically externalized his heart and lung function. While on the machine, he hadn't shown any sign of turning around, and you can only be on ECMO for so long. It was time to face the truth. The most extreme intervention the hospital could offer hadn't worked. The palliative care doctor came in and explained how, once they took him off the ECMO machine, they would make their baby comfortable as he passed. How they would be able to hold him and say goodbye.

Their baby boy.

This is an absurdity not unlike the suicide of a friend.

The next morning, I had to drive for hours from the hospital to a preaching engagement. A storm had just passed through, and the light in the sky had an otherworldly quality to it. The landscape radiated strangely with that same radical luminescence I saw in San Diego, and I wept in the car.

But here's the thing: Their baby boy hadn't died that night, and he's thriving now. When I set out on that drive, I knew Theo had survived. The night before, I had begun to grieve with Rick and Chelsea as they prepared themselves to say goodbye to their precious son. But when they took Theo off the ECMO machine, his vitals miraculously improved. When I made that drive, I wasn't weeping at a loss, but at the sheer depth of presence I sensed in everything around me.

I've wondered in those moments, did the environment change, or had my vision changed? Were my surroundings extraordinary, or through mourning had I consented to a brief but extraordinary capacity to see?

I suspect that mourning—especially intentionally chosen acts of grief, or any time we choose to render absence visible through ritual—fortifies that capacity within. Whether we hold a funeral, or write a letter to that which was lost, or erect a monument, or paddle out on the water to say goodbye, these acts that give witness to loss simultaneously heighten our perception of wholeness and so bring healing.

Of course, it's not the only feeling. There's also numbness and anger and defeat. But there is that tenderness we discover in the wake of grief. It's as if the soul is an eye that sees more than what our actual eyes see, and acts of mourning dilate the soul, letting in more light. The same inner place that is stricken with loss is then overwhelmed with the glory that cannot be diminished. And so we praise.

———

This isn't just about personal loss, though. It's about collective loss, too. The blessing for the mourners is for all of us who see the public, systemic matters we're facing, and it calls for acts of public lament.

This is why we build memorials like the one at Ground Zero in New York City.

This is why we hold candlelight vigils after mass shootings.

This is why we say the names of those lost in the unjust and discriminatory use of power. Theirs are not expendable bodies but rather sacred vessels of the glory of God. If we do not mourn, we run the risk of dampening this glory-knowing capacity within, making it even easier to commit such heinous acts of desecration again. Lives become disposable when we fail to see the glory in them. This blessing for the act of mourning is wisdom for a whole society that wants to heal.

———

And so while the loss isn't blessed—it's horrible, it's hell—the mourning is. When we mourn, we are given a strange access to the Wholeness underneath and within everything that can never be fragmented. And with a knowledge of that Wholeness, we can work to put things back together.

The comfort that Jesus promises for the mourners—I don't think it's a sentimental "there, there," or the false comfort of denial. I think it's this mystery: That in naming the very real things we've lost, we are given access to an experience of the undiminished wholeness that we are always swimming in.

I'm not suggesting that every funeral should lead to a

mystical experience. But even if you don't notice a luminescence in the landscape, I think Jesus knows that in lament
and mourning—that in turning toward our grief—we are also
turning toward the deep within us and making it more likely
that we will revel in the deep around us again.

4

THE REAL IS GIVEN, NEVER TAKEN

Blessed are the meek,
for they will inherit the earth.

I have a friend named Angela who's as bright and impressive as anyone you've ever met. She's a leader in our church. She became a part of our core team from our very first days, and since then, she's preached, led the communion team, and helped us show up better and more bravely as a majority white church trying to take seriously the call for our commitment to racial justice. She's a Black woman with a PhD and a professor who directs a graduate program at the University of Notre Dame. She's not superhuman, but to spend almost any time with her is to realize she's a person of tremendous strength. If you really get to know her, though, and learn from her experience, you'll hear story after story of environments she has lived and worked in that didn't have a place for her or her strength.

There was the time she was being measured for her gown for graduation, which would include all the regalia that indicate her advanced degrees. The person doing the measuring kept insisting that she needed to be fitted for a housekeeping uniform. She had to patiently explain that she was a member of the faculty. It defied their expectations that a Black woman could fit that category. There have been slights from students and snubs from colleagues. The list goes on and on. What I've understood in theory has become more real in friendship as she has helped me appreciate just how powerfully a system can set itself up against the strength of a person whose race or gender disqualifies them from its implicit ideals.

Sometimes all the strength in the world can do you no good. It's not that your strength has been robbed. It's been rendered irrelevant. The very gifts and assets you've been given that are meant to help you secure your place in the world, meant to help you take for yourself the things you need, have been somehow neutralized. It's as if you've been given great wealth in one form of currency, and it's not that your money has been taken. It's just that the system decided it no longer accepts it. They trade on bitcoin and you're holding cash. This often happens in a broken world. And this is the kind of experience I hear Jesus describing when he offers his next blessing.

———

Jesus blesses "the meek, for they shall inherit the earth."

In English, the word *meek* can mean humility. It can refer to a person who governs their own strength or who restrains their own anger. In Matthew's gospel, the same Greek word used here in the Beatitude that's translated as *meek* is later used when Jesus calls out to people who are weary and burdened. In that invitation, most English translations have him describing himself as "gentle." In these uses, it sounds like we've gone from the experience of sufferers described in the first two Beatitudes to a posture of virtue. And to be clear, many of the predominant interpretations see this Beatitude as a blessing for people who manage to control themselves.

But if you'll continue to allow me to offer my own experience of these Beatitudes, I want to reach back to another thread of interpretation that corresponds to an all too familiar experience for all of us when the world breaks.

————

The word for *meek* in Greek is *praus*, and an older use of the word *praus* leads us to an interpretation of this blessing that describes the strange disempowerment that comes when your power or strength isn't taken, but it's rendered useless.

The history comes from the training of horses for different tasks in the ancient world—everything from pulling wagons to racing to war. These horses were brought into training from the wild, which means they had to be tamed. A Greek philosopher and military leader named Xenophon wrote a whole book about the training of horses, and in it he said:

"If you want to correct a spirited horse when he is going too fast, do not pull him suddenly, but quietly check him with the bit, *soothing* him to a quiet pace."* The word translated *soothing* here has the same root as *praus*. This horse has been made meek.

————

* Xenophon, *On the Art of Horsemanship.*

73

This horse hasn't been made weak. It isn't deficient in spirit or courage. Xenophon literally describes the horse as "spirited." And it hasn't simply chosen of its own accord to tame itself. Its strength has been bridled. Anyone who has suffered deeply knows what this feels like.

———

I saw this bridled spirit in the Beqaa Valley of Lebanon not too long ago. It was the early days of the war in Syria, and millions of refugees had fled, many of them ending up in neighboring Lebanon. I traveled there with a nonprofit that was providing crisis relief. I was eager to see the work they were doing, especially because our church was considering supporting their work. But I was more eager to meet these refugees. By this point in life, I had learned that the closer we are to the breaking points in the world, the more likely we are to stumble into the deep Reality that reveals itself in those moments. I had seen over and over again how the Spirit had shown herself in the breaking points. How God had raised up wisdom in people who had watched the world collapse around them. The trip felt like a pilgrimage, but the holy sites I was looking for wouldn't be enshrined in ancient stones. They would be found in the makeshift tents of Syrians who had been chased out of their homeland by the violence there.

If you had asked me on my way to Lebanon what I expected, or what I imagined when I pictured these refugees, I would have pleaded ignorance. I would have told you I don't know any Syrian people. I've never been to Lebanon. I would have told you I assume they, like any humans facing the extreme disruption of displacement, are probably having a hard time. Other than that, I would have thought my assumptions were a clean slate. But when I first began meeting them, the surprise I felt at the stories I heard convicted me and showed me the biases I had.

Before we arrived at the first tented encampment, we were briefed on the situation there and some of the security risks involved with our trip. This was very close to ISIS-held territory, at a time when ISIS was showing a lot of strength and an appetite for aggressive territorial expansion. Westerners were attractive hostages for ISIS, so in addition to our security briefing, we were required to fill out some paperwork that included questions whose answers were very personal and specific. It was a little like the security questions you might answer for your online bank—ways you can prove it's really you who's trying to log in. The reason we had to fill out this part of the paperwork, it was explained to us, was that if any of us were taken hostage by ISIS, they could use these questions to force ISIS to verify whether we were really alive or dead. If they asked ISIS to get an answer from a hostage, and the answer came back accurate, it would prove the hostage was still alive. This was unnerving to say the least. It also fed my arrogant American assumptions about the gap between the world I had come from and the world I was in over there.

After the briefing, we traveled to an encampment where thousands of displaced Syrians were living. I don't know what image you have in mind when I tell you that, but I'm guessing it's not what we saw. Somehow these refugees had fashioned real homes out of tarps and two-by-fours. You felt you were in a neighborhood. There were courtyards and patios outlined with cinderblocks and remnants of rebar typically used to reinforce concrete. Their tented homes had bedrooms and living rooms and beautiful rugs covering the dusty floors. We were graciously invited into one of these tented homes by a family and asked to sit and talk. The father spoke eloquent English. He told us his story. He was a surgeon with a thriving medical practice in Syria. When the war broke out, they were committed to staying. After all, if everyone left, Syria would simply fall into the hands of those who were destroying it. They felt their best act of resistance was to continue to live their lives in the midst of a war zone.

This was where I began to feel embarrassed—no, that's too weak a word—I was mortified at my arrogance, at my prejudiced assumptions about the people I would meet on this trip. I said a second ago that if you had asked me what I imagined when I thought of these refugees, I would have said I really wasn't sure. But the fact is, when this gentleman, speaking in clear English, told me about his medical practice, I was surprised. My reaction was the tell. I had never thought that the first refugee I met would have been a surgeon. For me, *refugee* was a category with implicit, unnamed assumptions, and

76

somewhere on that list of expectations was the idea that they wouldn't be that educated. That they wouldn't have that kind of professional gravitas. I'm still embarrassed about it as I write this right now.

As he told us about his medical practice, and about their family's commitment to staying in Syria to resist the war, one of his daughters came out and brought us tea. She might have been twelve years old. We were in an improvised tent in a valley not far from a bloody war, but you would have thought we were sitting for tea time in a posh neighborhood in London based on the care with which we were served. I was reeling from the confrontation between my implicit assumptions about the kinds of weaknesses I would find in that valley, and the kind of strength I discovered when I got there.

But then the father explained why they finally left. He said that they lived in a city apartment building with many floors above them, and at night they would hear helicopters flying overhead dropping barrel bombs. These are savage instruments of indiscriminate violence. Oil drums filled with explosives and metal fragments, dropped in residential areas to kill civilians. These bombs had landed on their building, decimating the floors above them, and one night they realized there weren't many floors left before their home would be the one destroyed in an attack. The father looked at us and for a moment lost his composure as he distilled their decision to flee. "When you realize you can no longer protect your children if you remain, it is time to leave."

This was meekness as I've come to understand it. There was nothing weak about this man or his family. I sensed his strength in every way. The strength of his character. The strength of his intellect. The strength of his desire to resist the war. The strength of his love for his family. And yet, with all that strength, here he was in a tented encampment, he and his family dependent on the aid of Western nonprofits showing up with water and hygiene stations in a crowded valley. The circumstances of a broken world had bridled him and he was no longer able to secure for himself and his family the things they needed.

———

This is where this blessing surprises and subverts. Jesus assumes a fundamentally different system from the one we're living in. Our system, the one we've found ourselves in and the one we keep perpetuating, is a system where you have what you need if you're able to take it for yourself. It's survival of the fittest. It's each man or woman for himself or herself. It's a world of the haves and the have-nots, and the goal is to have, which means the goal is to learn how to take. This leads to violence, because in the system I've described, the methods used for taking will inevitably, endlessly escalate.

The prizes go to the ones who are best at taking. This is the case for individuals and families and it's the operating assumption of whole economies and empires. It's hard to overstate just how deeply entrenched this view of things is. If you're trying to take care of yourself or your family, you'd better learn how to play along, because the world belongs to those who are able to take it by force. But in spite of how deeply formed we are in this way of seeing and acting, Jesus doesn't see it that way.

————

Most scholars who study this blessing agree that Jesus must have had Psalm 37 in mind when he offered it:

> *A little while, and the wicked will be no more;*
> *though you look for them, they will not be found.*
> *But the meek will inherit the land*
> *and enjoy peace and prosperity.*

The meek will inherit the land. Those whose strength is bridled will receive everything. But all of this will happen in...a little while.

Will it? How long is a little while? It sure seems like this system we have right now has held sway for a very, very long time.

One way of interpreting these blessings is that they look forward to a time in the future where God will reorder everything. The technical term for this way of reading is *eschatological*. Christian hope has always included a view toward the future that sees God dealing with injustice and setting things right.

But theologians also speak of a *partially realized eschatology*. That's a technical way of saying that the good future we hope for is already here somehow, coexisting alongside and within the broken world. It's a way of noticing that the current arrangements that may seem powerful and inevitable are already being subverted if you're paying attention. It's a way of hoping that's more than a belief about the future—it's a capacity to see the fragility in the seemingly enduring arrangements that have made some of us meek. I think Jesus saw the fragility in these arrangements, and maybe that shaped his conviction that there's another arrangement that would overcome the current one.

———

Let's talk about that fragility. In the movie *Wall Street: Money Never Sleeps*, Shia LaBeouf plays a promising young investment banker in the world of New York City's high-powered financiers. There's a scene where he meets with one of the power players, portrayed by Josh Brolin, and he asks Brolin a question:

"What's your number?"

Brolin's character misunderstands the question and tells LaBeouf about the starting salary at his firm. LaBeouf clarifies:

"No no no. *Your* number. The amount of money you would need to just walk away from it and live. See, I find that everybody has a number and it's usually an exact number, so what is yours?"

And then Brolin's character gives a one-word answer that expresses a whole world view. It expresses an entire pathology. It sums up the system we're living in, and it shows how crazy, how fragile, how unsustainable it is. It shows that no one is satisfied when they play by the rules of this system. It shows that taking, no matter how good you are at it, no matter how much power you have to use in its pursuit, doesn't satisfy. What's his answer?

"More."

It's one of the more believable moments in a movie with plenty of fantasy. It expresses the unresolved anxiety of the system that demands you to fight for everything you need. Brolin's character may seem powerful, but his answer reveals a deep fragility. Jesus doesn't believe it's a good or necessary posture, and I've often wondered if the early stories of his own people helped form that view in him.

———

The first mention of sin in Scripture isn't where you'd think it is. Between some passages in Paul's letters in the New Testament and some interpretations offered by Christian thinkers over the centuries, most of us have come to assume that the story of Adam and Eve eating the forbidden fruit and being expelled from the Garden of Eden would include the first mention of sin, but in fact the word never appears in that story. That doesn't necessarily mean the story isn't about sin. Good storytellers often get to the point without using the labels we expect. But the word never appears there.

The first mention of sin in Scripture happens in the next story, the one about their sons, Cain and Abel, that's told in Genesis 4. In that story, each brother brings a sacrifice to God that comes from his work. Abel kept flocks, so he brought fat portions from the firstborn of his flock, and Cain brought some of the fruits from the soil. The text says that "The Lord looked with favor on Abel and his offering, but on Cain and his offering he did not look with favor."

Cain gets angry about this, and God confronts him. He tells him that if he doesn't do what's right, sin is crouching at his door. (There's the first mention of sin that we've been waiting for.) Rather than heed the warning, Cain lures his little brother Abel out into a field, where he kills him.

What's this story about? Let's start with the two offerings. Some teachers will tell you that Abel's offering was better, indicated by the details of "fat portions" and "firstborn." Other teachers, taking a more historical-critical approach, will tell you that this story reflects a later preference among Israelites to uphold the virtue of shepherds, in line with their esteem for King David, who had been a shepherd before he took the throne.

In either of those interpretations, this ends up being a story about virtue and failure before God, and about God rewarding virtue and rejecting failure. However, if you pay close attention, you'll notice that the results of this whole thing don't really play by that logic (we'll say more about that in a bit).

There's another problem with both of those interpretations: A lot of scholars say that any perceived distinction between Cain's and Abel's sacrifices is just a distraction. A red herring. They say the whole point of this story begins in the idea that Cain and Abel don't really have any reason to think one of their sacrifices would be more accepted than the other. This may not be a story about how to show up at the altar with a sacrifice that God will approve of. Rather, this may be a story that asks the question: What do you do when someone else has the blessing?

It might be that the first mention of sin in Scripture comes up in a story that raises all the anxious questions we ask when it feels like there's only so much blessing to go around. Only so much goodness to receive. Only so much estate to inherit. And someone else is getting blessed, receiving the goodness, inheriting the estate.

———

The anxiety that Josh Brolin's character expresses with his unsatisfiable pursuit of more may not be that far removed from the anger Cain feels toward Abel. These are grasping, taking postures in a world where it feels like there's only so much to go around. If I'm right about the Genesis story, we might find this tale of jealousy and grasping repeated later in the story. And in fact that's what happens.

Take the story of Jacob and Esau for example. Here again

we have two brothers and a fight over the blessing. Esau is the older one, but Jacob has been a grasper from the moment he came out of the womb. When his older brother, the right recipient of his father's blessing and estate, is out doing his work, Jacob, conspiring with his mother, senses his opportunity and tricks his father into giving him the blessing instead.

I once had a professor say that you can understand the entire book of Genesis as a meditation on "the problem of chosenness." It's written by and for a people who simultaneously understand themselves as the chosen people of God and who have had so much taken from them throughout their history. And if you look closely at the narrative of chosenness—of scarce blessings being distributed—you'll see Genesis subverting all our assumptions about how this works.

In the story of Cain and Abel, it seems from the sacrifice story that Abel is the chosen one. But at the end of the story, while he lies dead in a field, his brother ends up living the rest of his days with a mark of protection over his life.

Later, Abraham has been given a promise of inherited land and ongoing blessing, but he wavers in his trust of that promise. A child is born from his flailing trust—an illegitimate son who, along with his mother, is sent away. Yet their roaming family is given a promise of their own, not unlike the promise given to Abraham—with ongoing descendants.

We've already talked about Jacob and Esau, so let's move on to Jacob and his twelve sons. He shows special favor to one of the youngest, Joseph. To have the patriarch's blessing is to enjoy a competitive advantage over your many brothers. And yet all that blessing does Joseph little good. He ends up thrown into a pit, then dragged down to Egypt as a slave, then locked up in prison. Eventually he's raised up to a position of extreme power, controlling all the resources of Egypt as their people endure a famine. But his father and brothers and whole family end up benefitting from his position when they come into the land to provide for themselves.

If you watch these stories closely, you can see them using the logic of chosenness and inheritance subversively. Now, I know that chosenness and inheritance may not be categories that many of us think within these days. If we get a raise at work, or if we enjoy a secure existence, we may think of it as a blessing, but most of us don't think of ourselves as the specially chosen daughters and sons at the expense of siblings who we imagine have been rejected by God.

But if you understand these ideas of chosenness and inheritance as the containers these storytellers used to carry the freight of our anxieties about scarcity and provision, it's not too hard to find ourselves connecting to them. And if we do that, we might discover that we're being coaxed into a different imagination about how it is that we will get our hands on the things we need.

———

I had my own complicated relationship with Notre Dame. It wasn't complicated by the dynamics of race and gender that

Angela deals with, but it had its own anxieties. I grew up here near campus, and I idolized that place. I'll never forget the first football game I went to as a kid with my dad. The whole campus felt to me like another world. As a bookish kid with a love for architecture and nature, it's like the place was made for me. However, I wasn't made for it. At least not as an undergraduate.

I didn't have the grades or the money for Notre Dame. A few of my friends did, though. I ended up at another college here in the same area. I would visit my friends at Notre Dame and, walking across campus back to my car at the end of the night, feel almost sick to my stomach at the fact that I didn't have what it took to attain access to that place.

But I remember one day walking the campus and realizing the foolishness of what I was feeling. I asked myself what it was that I found so compelling about Notre Dame. The first thought that came to mind was the beauty of the campus. I was literally walking the campus, with full access to that beauty, as I had been hanging my head for not being a student there. I thought about the intellectual resources I wanted access to, but my favorite intellectual resources aren't classrooms; they're libraries. The college I attended had an agreement with Notre Dame that allowed me to check out anything from their library. I thought about the spirituality of the environment at Notre Dame—statues and mosaics of Jesus and a grotto with candles that helped me pray, and a basilica that rivaled the historic cathedrals of Europe—and how I was regularly taking advantage of all those features of the environment that were available for anyone.

The things I'm talking about—beauty, knowledge, spirit—they're not the kinds of things that can be held captive. Beauty always has a way of breaking out. Knowledge tends to spread even when it's censored. Spirit is by definition not the kind of thing that can be controlled. However, they *are* the kinds of things that can be missed when we're fixated on other kinds of things. The kinds of things that are freely given—the kinds of things that are sourced in grace, like beauty and knowledge and spirit—are hard to receive when our hands are grasping. Ideally, we would open our hands and cease our grasping through intentionality and spiritual practice, but when our grasping is defeated by a broken world whose systems and circumstances are set against us, maybe the blessing is the way those moments teach us to receive.

———

I don't think it's bad for us to work for the things we need. I don't think it's bad for us to build our skills and exercise our power for our own benefit. This is the basic work of building a life. There's a real dignity in seeing your own effort return to you in having your needs met and your life secured.

But there's such a fine line between working hard for the things you need and the grasping that characterizes our lives. Taking and grasping are closed-handed postures. They require our fingers to grip tightly, to get locked in a white-knuckled possession of everything we think we need. This is a pretty good description of the way most of us most of the time relate to the world around us. It makes it harder to give. But, perhaps even more tragically, it makes it harder to receive.

Jesus gave his followers one specific practice to help us continually return to his death and resurrection—one specific practice to go deeper and deeper into the meaning and hope of his own life: the Eucharist. This is the sacred meal that Christians around the world have been celebrating together since the very first days of our movement. In this meal, we often say that one cannot take the Eucharist. It can only be received. There is no grasping at the table with Jesus. Only open-handed trust.

What we inherit in the family Jesus establishes is not some material blessing. Not a bigger check on payday. The thing we inherit—the blessing we receive—is the gift of Godself. It's not unlike what we've already heard with the first two blessings. The prize we have access to when we suffer is the life of God in us.

If it's true that a white-knuckled, grasping hand is incapable of receiving, then the only way we inherit is if somehow our hands are opened up again. I would hope that we could learn this posture intentionally, through practices that lead us away from fragility and anxiety and into trust. But maybe the surprising blessing of a broken world is that even when its circumstances or systems bridle our strength and keep us from the pursuit of more, we can find ourselves provided for in all the ways that matter most.

I think back to my friend Angela, or the Syrian family I met in Lebanon. The circumstances they're both facing are wrong and should be resisted. This isn't a suggestion that people who inhabit broken systems and circumstances shouldn't fight for the reformation of those things.

However, Jesus seems to think that the Real, the Good, the True, the Beautiful, the things that sustain us beyond flesh and blood, are available to us even when we're bound up. I've come to believe that so much of what I admire about Angela and others like her, and that so much of what I found admirable and powerful in the lives of the Syrians I met in Lebanon, was that the meekness they endured had given them access to a deeper stream of provision that's waiting for all of us if we'll just stop grasping and open our hands.

5

THE HUNGER IS
THE FEAST

Blessed are those who hunger and thirst
for righteousness,
    for they will be filled.

Back in 2010, when I was in the middle of my time in the West Bank, stumbling into these strange blessings after ruminating on that dark mantra that "there's no way this gets better," I began to recognize something familiar in the experience I was having. Sitting next to such intense suffering, I was vaguely in touch with something else in my life that had felt like this, but I couldn't pin it down right away. Like a familiar smell that you know is connected to a memory, even if you can't remember what it is.

To sit next to suffering is its own cross to bear. The actual suffering is its own awful thing, of course. This isn't comparative. But to walk alongside someone while they struggle to find their way, or while they are rocked by circumstances, is a distinct kind of hardship. It brings its own kind of despair. It raises unique questions of hope, because your heart is being dragged through the pain of a situation in which you have no agency. Or at least it seems that way.

My reaction to everything I was seeing and learning on the trip kept vacillating between fight or flight. One minute I'm raging inside, trying to think of anywhere I could direct my energy to push back against the situation. The next minute I would want to retreat. To numb out. To put as much distance as possible between me and the pain I was witnessing. I remember pacing the streets in a refugee camp after seeing that footage of the kids' playground being attacked with tear gas canisters that I mentioned in the first chapter, feeling frantic with that restless vacillation in my body as part of me wanted to rip something apart and another part of me wanted to run.

One of the truly beautiful and terrible things about being human is our capacity to sense the gap between what is and what should be. We experience it not as some cold, calculated analysis. We feel it in our guts. In our bones. The feeling robs us of sleep. Robs us of peace. I think this capacity goes back to the soul. It runs deeper than our emotions, although it's felt emotionally. It's more than physiology, although it can make our heart race and muscles clench. It's such a terrible thing to abide that it generates that fight-or-flight feeling—we have to do something to resolve the feeling. But something holy opens up in us when we are able to be present to it while it remains unresolved. This posture—staying present while it's unresolved—was another part of the strange familiarity I was sensing on the trip.

So I tried to process the experience with the Palestinians and Israelis and at the same time figure out what was so familiar about it. And then I slowly realized what it was. There had been another situation in my life that had persisted for years where I was close to someone else's suffering and at a total loss for how to deal with it.

———

I spent years in close relationship with someone in the throes of addiction. I say "spent" because, thank God, he's been sober now for quite a while. He's one of the most transformed people I've ever known. I have the privilege of learning from him and the path he's on in his recovery, and I often benefit from the wisdom he shares with me. If you have friends in recovery, learn from them. And if you're in recovery, know that we all need the wisdom you're gaining as you keep walking forward one day at a time. You're often the ones among us most advanced and aware. You're tapping into truths that speak to all of us in our own healing and growth.

So things are really good now. But there were a lot of years when it was hell.

There were the nights in college when I kept my phone close to my bed in case he would call in the middle of the night with a crisis.*

There were the days when I tried to come up with something wise or insightful to say that might help, and those days usually ended up with me putting my foot in my mouth.

There were the long stretches where I wouldn't hear from him and would wonder if he was dead or alive.

There was the time I went to stay with him and didn't

———

* This was just long enough ago that it wasn't normal for people to keep their cell phones next to their bed. Funny how we forget that we haven't always been this way.

understand until we were walking into his house that he was living with his dealer at the time.

There were the short pilgrimages I would make to the grotto on Notre Dame's campus where I would light a candle and kneel to pray for him, desperate for something that would help me feel like my prayers were going somewhere.

To love someone struggling with addiction is to stand on the shore watching them being dragged out by a rip current. There are moments that seem to last forever as they're pulled under and you lose sight, assuming they've drowned. Other moments where you see them struggling against the current, kicking and paddling with everything they've got, but still overwhelmed by the power of the water. You're screaming at them, as if anything you could offer from the shore could make a difference. You hope they can at least hear you over the crashing surf, can at least understand that you're keeping your eye on them, as if that does them any good. You're looking around for a lifeguard but they're nowhere to be found. You find yourself thinking, were we not prepared for this? Where's the Coast Guard? Isn't there some show of force, some summoning of human power, that could make us invincible to situations like this? You call all the experts on rip currents, you read their books, and then you look back out to the water and realize their analysis isn't going to help you right now. Against your better judgment, you even enter the water, try to grab them and drag them back, but it's too violent out there. You're not trained for this. They slip out of your grip. The cruelty of this experience is hard to state, both for the one out there in the water and the others on the shore watching their loved one get dragged away.

You think back and try to figure out how and when a pleasant day at the beach turned into this hellish scene, as if understanding how we got here could fix things right now. When someone you love slips into addiction, one of the strange things about it is that you don't always know when it became addiction. You might not even have that word for what they're going through. They might not have named it yet. This means your brain doesn't have a clinical word or category for what's going on. You just have the screaming inside telling you that things should not be this way.

Jesus has a blessing for people who hear the screaming inside, who know in their bodies and brains and feelings and souls that there's a gap between what is and what should be. And while I hadn't connected to this blessing through most of the years that I'm describing here, it all began to come together as I tracked down that familiar feeling in the West Bank.

———

Here's the promise for people who hear the screaming inside: "Blessed are those who hunger and thirst for righteousness, for they will be filled." Jesus gives a blessing for people aching for things to be right.

The word *righteousness* is a tricky one these days. We talk more about "self-righteousness" than "righteousness," and we don't mean something positive when we say it. I think our negative feelings about self-righteousness are connected to the baggage a lot of us are carrying related to pious, moralistic religion. I've heard preaching that had me convinced that I just need to feel bad about my failures, and sometimes the failures the preachers seemed to have in mind were pretty trite. It's like they thought their job was to generate a shameful feeling in me about the fact that I liked dirty jokes or had hormones or found swear words captivating. Or if I could only beat my own brow enough, I might stop dreaming about things as self-ish as making music for a living and instead make myself a missionary or martyr. Surely that was the righteous life, and the people Jesus was blessing were the people who wanted it. I didn't want it.

You live a little longer, though, and you discover your capacity for destruction. You look at your own life, or the world around you, and you see a crime scene with your fingerprints all over it. In spite of those trite, shaming preachers doing their best to make this small and petty, you begin to realize that you've helped create the gap between the way things are and the way they should be. You taste the bitterness of your own unrighteousness.

We do in fact live consequential lives, whether we realize it or not. We're stewards of our own energies, decision makers for what to do with our time, our bodies, our words, our hab-its, and when we get those decisions wrong, suffering can be unleashed in the world. Whether we like it or not, to be human is high stakes. Sometimes the screaming inside is a response to our own inability to live up to a standard that really matters. Righteousness and unrighteousness are good categories for when we face the dark possibilities of what we can be.

Still, at this point we're looking at the self, and all those years walking with someone else through their own self-destruction brought me in touch with questions that are bigger than the self.

———

The thing that made someone else's struggle with addiction into an experience of suffering for me was love. This was happening to someone I love. Without love, someone else's suffering doesn't become your own. It's why you can gawk at a tragedy but not necessarily suffer because of it. It's why we can scroll through feeds with painful images and harrowing videos and, while these feeds have our attention, and they might even disturb us, we don't actually suffer through them. Voyeurs don't suffer when others suffer. Lovers do.

Love is more than a feeling. It's more than an act. It's an opening of the heart to the truth of our connection. It's a frequency we tune into that has us resonating on the same wavelength.

This love is the way that we're called to be with one another—not just family or close friends, but the whole human family. It's the foundation of Jesus's worldview. It invites us into an expanding awareness of all the ways we belong to one another. Of course, with that expansion of belonging, the screaming inside might increase as we become aware of whole systems and structures that aren't working.

I've been using the word *righteousness* for the thing we hunger and thirst for. That's a translation of the Greek word *dikaiosune* that Matthew uses here. But there's another way it can be translated: *justice*. If those who hunger and thirst for righteousness are craving for things to be right within their own lives, you could say the hunger and thirst for justice is a craving for things to be right between us and all around us. This isn't just a blessing for us as we bump up against our capacity for self-destruction. It's also a blessing for all who suffer injustice at the hands of others or as a consequence of an unfair system.

This is a blessing for Black lives that matter in a world designed with the assumption that they don't. It's a blessing for refugees whose homelands have been turned into wastelands by the powers of empires that have treated them like collateral damage in their quest for domination. It's a blessing for women who have had to play along with the patriarchy. It's a blessing for anyone who wakes up and discovers that we have so far to go and that we're actually all in this together.

———

So, in talking about righteousness or justice, we can expand beyond the self to talk about us, about the things we do and the world we create together. However, in the Bible, more than righteousness is about me or us, it's a category for God. It's about whether God will live up to the things God said God will do. It's about people liberated but wandering, wondering when they're going to get to come home. It's about people who've been promised God's presence, but who feel an absence where they thought God would be. You could say righteousness is a covenant word. It's a word for making good on a promise.

Job says of God:

> "The Almighty is beyond our reach and exalted in power; in his justice and great righteousness, he does not oppress."*

In other words, because we trust that God is righteous, we can expect God to do the right thing.

The poet in Psalm 71 says:

"In your righteousness, rescue me and deliver me; turn your ear to me and save me."

In other words, God, I'm expecting you to show up in a way that's consistent with who you are.

In Isaiah 46, a prophet speaking to people in exile, people living in the consequences of their own destructive decisions, hears God saying:

"I am bringing my righteousness near, it is not far away; and

---

* Job 37:23.

my salvation will not be delayed. I will grant salvation to Zion, my splendor to Israel."

And the reason writers like Paul in the New Testament make such a big deal out of righteousness is that they found God living up to God's promises through their experience of Jesus.

I point this out because these strange blessings have been bent over and over again into prescriptions for behavior, and I don't think that's where they start. With this fourth blessing, I still think we're in the realm of grace and gift. I don't think this is a command to make ourselves righteous. I don't even think it's a mandate to do the work of justice. (Don't get me wrong—you can find that mandate all over Scripture. God clearly wants us to do the work of justice. I just don't think that's what's happening here.)

Not only do I not see a command to make ourselves righteous here, as if we could climb up into the Divine; I don't even see a command to make ourselves crave righteousness, as if we could generate such a desire by will. I think Jesus believes that the desire is already with us, and it just needs to be welcomed. Uncovered. Embraced. That's the subversive effect of the blessing. It's not a command. It's a gentle invitation to stop filling our empty bellies with empty calories. It's an invitation to realize we have been guzzling toxic chemicals in an effort to slake our thirst. If we stop for a moment, we may realize that though we have consumed so much, we're still hungry. We're still thirsty.

———

In the last chapter, we talked about eschatology, and how these blessings are sometimes read as a forward-looking promise to a future that the book of Revelation describes when it talks about a new heaven and a new earth, a time when God will wipe every tear from our eyes, a time when evil will be permanently defeated. A time when the world is put back together and will never break again.

But I'm trying to tell you that there's another way these blessings work. A more surprising possibility. A way of working that has the power to ground our hope in the here and now. With this blessing, we might discover that what we crave most deeply is actually felt *in* our hunger, *in* our thirst.

Cynthia Bourgeault is an Episcopal priest who defines the righteousness of God like this: "To be 'in the righteousness of God'...means to be anchored within God's own aliveness... Jesus promises that when the hunger arises within you to find your own deepest aliveness within God's aliveness, it will be satisfied—in fact, *the hunger itself is a sign that the bond is already in place*"* (italics mine). yes - amen -

The hunger itself is a sign that the bond is already in place. In the here and now, the "aliveness" of God that Bourgeault is naming might actually be the thing we feel when we're hungry. Dead things do not hunger and thirst. Hunger and thirst

---

* *The Wisdom Jesus*, pg. 44.

are signs of life. Metabolism is literally a sign that your flesh is alive. You're breathing, consuming, burning energy every moment. If you weren't, something would be wrong with you.

I've come to believe that the hunger and thirst I feel for things to be right—either within me or around me—is itself an aliveness. A waking up. A sign of the Divine presence. And if righteousness is the substance of God, then perhaps, paradoxically, the hunger is a sign that I am being filled with the thing I crave.

Bourgeault goes on: "As we enter the path of transformation, the most valuable thing we have working in our favor is our yearning. Some spiritual teachers will even say that the yearning you feel for God is actually coming from the opposite direction; it is in fact God's yearning for *you*."*

———

Here's one more way of saying it: The gap we feel between the way things are and the way things should be is something we would only feel if *the way things should be is somehow already with us.* Think about it: For any tension to exist, both components that hold the tension must be present. If the only thing that's with us, that's in us, is *the broken-down condition of the way things are right now,* then there's no tension there. The tension exists because something else—the aliveness, the righteousness—is with us, too.

———

* Ibid.

The future we long for is somehow with us. Incomplete, for sure. But with us. And if we can learn to trust that the feast we long for is with us, we may stop filling our bellies with empty calories and slaking our thirst with toxic chemicals. When we do, we discover that the craving, the aching, the screaming inside, is something like an instinct that we can hold on to, pay attention to, and that the instinct will help us find our way to the feast.

I know a lot of addiction stories don't end well. I know a lot of conflict and occupation stories keep getting worse, not better. I don't mean to sound naïve. But I don't think Jesus was naïve when he told us to trust the hunger, to abide the thirst, because he had already tasted the feast.

This is one of the best descriptions / articulations of how much God loves us + the amazing way he woos us + loves us to Him —

— The tension, frustration, longing for the world to be a better place IS the Spirit of God —

He will redeem it all as we trust Him —

6

THE TURN

At this point, Jesus has blessed us in some of the most difficult things we experience. He hasn't blessed the circumstances that create these inner aches. He hasn't called us to resign ourselves in the face of a broken world. But he has blessed us by naming what happens in the world within us when the world around us breaks.

I hope you feel truly seen by these blessings. When you've had your spirit robbed; when you've lost something you treasured; when your power has been bridled by circumstance or the system; when you've craved a reordering of things in your life or the world, you know how lonely these experiences can be. How unseen they can leave you feeling. But you're not unseen. Jesus describes these experiences at the beginning of his central treatise in one of the gospels.

But is that all that's going on in Jesus' opening riff? Is he simply expressing solidarity with us in our pain? It's powerful to have our suffering named, but is that all the further this goes?

———

For centuries, people who've studied these blessings have noticed a shift between the first four and the last four. The first four seem to be naming what happens in us when we suffer. These blessings don't address our agency. They don't prescribe a path. Like I've tried to say while talking about them, they do invite us into something. But the thing they invite us into is an experience that's been imposed on us whether we wanted it or not. This is what a broken world does to us, and Jesus doesn't want us to try to run away from that.

But the next four blessings describe people who show up in a certain kind of way. In the second half of the Beatitudes, Jesus turns his attention to the kind of people who put things back together: the merciful, the pure in heart, the peacemakers, the persecuted. (If you're wondering what persecution has to do with all of this, just hang on. It's the most surprising, hopeful thing he says in all these blessings, but we'll have to wait until we get to that blessing to see what I mean.)

Once you notice this shift, you might wonder if his audience has changed, but as far as we can tell, it hasn't. Matthew doesn't describe Jesus offering the first four blessings to one crowd and the second four blessings to another. It's not like he gathered up all the sad sufferers for some comfort and consolation and then turned and convened a totally different crowd of resilient up-and-comers to talk about a transformative way of moving forward. So what's going on here?

————

A couple of years ago a friend and member of our church emailed me. She's the kind of person I would describe as wide-awake. Engaged. Paying attention. She takes seriously the problems we're facing in our world. She knows we've built a world that privileges some while marginalizing others. She's also trying to figure out how to hold all that awareness without succumbing to the cynicism it might engender. She's someone I love learning from. In the middle of her email she said something that a lot of us have been feeling in recent years. Her email stood out to me because of how self-aware she was in what she described:

> "The more I invest in paying attention to the injustices of our world, the finer the line becomes between rage/passion/grief/hopelessness/conviction, etc. When I look at injustice, something inside me wants to wage war against it. This junk comes up. My internal posture feels a lot like the very thing I say I'm against or abhor. It is this overpower/crush something/diminish someone type of response."

Most of us can relate. When we suffer, or when we see others suffering, it's tempting to start by simply pretending we're fine and that things are fine. But when that stops working—when we get broken down enough to stop pretending that there's nothing wrong—if we're not careful we may end up reacting with the same energy that we're trying to resist. I think this is what she was talking about in the email.

Reactions reenact whatever they're responding to. That's

literally what the word means. This is why violence begets violence. Why the abused often become abusers. Why pain and suffering keep circulating in the world. Why family systems can become spirals of intensifying hurt. If all you have is the pain you've inherited, it's all you have to give back.

But Jesus is saying that when we suffer, *the pain isn't all we have*. We have the life of God. The glory. When everything is taken, we're still the inheritors of the earth. When we're famished for righteousness or justice, we're actually on our way to a feast. And it may be that the way we lay hold of the life of God is by facing the suffering.

If we don't abide these inner experiences—if we avoid them or resist them or try to numb them—we may be cutting ourselves off from the resources Jesus has in mind when he makes all of those promises. I don't think God withholds Godself when we avoid or resist. I think it's in the nature of God to always give Godself to us, but not to give in a way that overrides our will.

We have to consent. Not to the things happening around us, because so much of what we face should be resisted. Critiqued. Called out. But we have to consent to the experience within ourselves, because it's there whether we like it or not. And it's in the truth of our inner experience—not a denial of it—where God meets us, because of course if God is anything, God is Reality, which means God isn't easily found when we avoid it.

Pádraig Ó Tuama is an Irish poet, theologian, and moderator of conflict. For years he led a community in Northern

Ireland called Corrymeela, an organization that focuses on peace and reconciliation. While leading Corrymeela, he wrote a book of prayers that draws on the spiritual practices of that community. The morning prayer in his book has a line that strikes me every time I pray it:

*"We will live the life we are living."**

I know—it may not sound profound. At first it almost sounds redundant. But think about it. How much effort do we put into avoiding and escaping our lives, especially when we're suffering? And think about how much trouble is caused when we do that.

We live half-hearted for years and then wonder why we can't find our way back to our hearts when the vitality of spirit has almost entirely vanished. The casual drinking becomes problem drinking and pretty soon we have a destructive relationship with alcohol and it starts destroying us and others. The unhealed grief comes out sideways as misdirected anger, and unsuspecting victims pay the price. The injustices we've suffered but never named leave us resentful and untrusting, and we penalize people who have nothing to do with what happened to us.

Our denials always end up giving back to the world the very things that have wounded us, and then we wonder why the

---

* From *Daily Prayer with the Corrymeela Community*, by Pádraig Ó Tuama.

world keeps breaking. One of the deep, perennial truths that every page of history tells is that whatever we're fighting cannot be defeated by the power that created it. Our path to a different kind of power takes us into the deepest interior spaces of our own souls before leading us out of ourselves to act in the world, and Jesus' first blessings call us to that path.

This isn't just good psychology, though, even though I'm all for good psychology, and we can use as much of it as we can get. Jesus grounds these blessings in an encounter with God, as if to say that what's at stake, and what's on offer, is bigger than whatever's going on in our heads. He understands all of these particular experiences against the horizon of the infinite, and he sees that horizon not just beyond us but within us, too.

Not too long ago I went overseas to spend a week in silent retreat at a Benedictine monastery because I'm very spiritual.

I kid, I kid.

I went there because of something I had heard years earlier from someone who lived in one of those monasteries. His name was Cuthbert, and we were students together in a grad school class. Cuthbert was from Ireland, and he was a Benedictine monk, and once I discovered that, I asked him if I could buy him a beer and ask him questions about monastic life. I wasn't interested in taking that path myself, but I was so curious about what it was like.

We went out one night to an Irish pub because I couldn't resist the thought of drinking Guinness with my Irish friend, and I pummeled him with questions about monastic life. At some point in the conversation Cuthbert must have figured out that I was idolizing him, because he cut me off and told me something I didn't expect to hear. "Jason, I didn't become a monk because I'm so spiritual. I became a monk because I realized that while my soul longs to pray, I'm very bad at it, and I don't know how to pray without a community."

Those words have stuck with me for years. Prayer is complicated for me. I believe in it. I don't think you'll get very far in your life with God without it. I don't even think you'll get very far in your humanity without some version of it. I keep finding that my heroes usually have some practice of it (in many forms), regardless of whether they identify with a religious tradition or what words they would use to describe the Thing they pray to, if they would describe it as a Thing at all. But man, it just doesn't come very natural to me. So when Cuthbert shared what he shared, it lodged deep in me. It shaped my understanding of spiritual community. It helped me not be so judgmental of myself on the many days when prayer is really hard.

Those words were with me when I made my plan to travel to this monastery overseas, too.

I had come through a hard season. Leading a church during a pandemic has been harder than I ever imagined this job could be. In one simultaneous experience, our community became far more vulnerable and in need of care, and we lost access to

115

most of our best channels to deal with all of those needs. When we could gather on Sundays, we could pray together. Lament together. We could look each other in the eyes, embrace each other, listen to each other. As a pastoral team, we could gauge the overall health and hurts of our church family each Sunday morning while we were all together. People naturally share the details of their lives when we gather that they keep to themselves when we're not together, so when we're together we hear about needs that can be materially addressed. And then, with the arrival of COVID-19, we lost that gathering. I told people it felt a little like we were driving a bus with the whole congregation loaded onto it. And in this metaphor, the situation is something like the movie *Speed* where we have to keep the bus moving. But then, while still having to keep driving, it was as if a dense fog hit the road and I couldn't see past the front of the bus, and a curtain dropped behind me and I couldn't see the passengers. It was a challenge unlike anything I had ever experienced in my work.

However, leading a church through the political division and unrest of the last few years has been even harder. Everyone seems hypervigilant and afraid that their church will become a place that sees you through the lens of who you voted for rather than the wholeness of who you are. Each week brings stories in the news that, if you don't address them, will have you called out by one group within the church, and if you do, will make you suspicious in the eyes of another.

After all of this, I sensed a spiritual weariness. I could feel a longing to pray, but I was having a hard time responding to the longing. So I traveled to this monastery hoping that being around a silent community of prayer would help me respond to that longing.

————

The only conversations I had on an otherwise silent retreat occurred during one hour each evening with one of the monks. He was an exceptional pastor for me while I was there. I shared with this brother some of the frustrating dynamics I find myself facing in my life and work. Even as I talked to him about it, I could feel the reactivity in me. I was feeling a lot of angst about some of the situations I was facing, and I was annoyed with the way some people were acting. I felt like there was a lot of immaturity I was having to deal with, and that other people's issues were getting projected on me in a way that was both unproductive and unfair.

He listened with a kind of compassion I've rarely seen on someone's face. He asked a few clarifying questions. Then he affirmed my frustration. He seemed to deeply understand the impossibility of the challenges I was facing. He had sympathy for the disheartened feeling I was carrying from all the baggage that other people had been throwing at me. It felt so good to have someone hear me and see me and tell me I wasn't crazy.

But then he got quiet for a moment. It's hard to say for how long because your awareness of time really gets funny when you spend days on end without any devices or demands. After that silent moment, he came back to me, and with that same deep compassion on his face, he told me: "I think that maybe the reason you're here is to explore the space within you. We all have a large interior that we rarely explore. When we inhabit only a small part of our own inner world, we tend to get reactive to the outer world. I think you need to ask why all of this is getting to you, and I think the solution is for you to spend some time exploring parts of your inner world that have gone neglected. You're here to meet God in those spaces."

This was not what I wanted to hear, but he was exactly right. After I spent a few minutes resisting what he was saying, I thought of a very different kind of monastic experience I had years earlier in life, and how it totally confirmed what he was telling me that day about my need to meet God in the neglected interior as a way of interacting productively with everything around me.

———

The earlier monastic experience happened when I was twenty-two years old. This was four years after that devastating eruption of traumatic memories from childhood that I described when I talked about the poor in spirit in chapter 2. The monastic experience I'm talking about didn't happen at a monastery, though. It happened in a psychiatric ward.

I spent my college years vacillating between seasons of denial about the pain I was in and seasons where I would try to attend to it. I would start seeing a therapist and we would work through the memories for a bit, but it seemed like every time I tried to pay attention to this stuff, the worse things got. What felt like an empty place inside on good days seemed more like a cosmic black hole inside that would swallow me up and leave nothing behind on bad days, and therapy days always ended up being bad days. So after a fresh stretch in therapy, I would opt out and try to get back to making it through life without help. That would work for a little while before it stopped working, and then I would go back to therapy again.

We tried everything. Talk therapy. EMDR.* Prayer and theology about healing and love. Journaling. I would read books about childhood trauma and try to understand myself. And then I would turn away and just try to pretend I was fine.

But each cycle of turning to therapy and turning away seemed to make things worse. Time wasn't healing anything. It was just allowing things to fester.

By the time I got to my senior year of college, I couldn't sustain a normal relationship with the world around me. I was failing my classes and lashing out at my friends. I would have to walk out of rooms or pull my car over when driving because I would randomly start crying so hard that I couldn't see the

---

* Eye movement desensitization and reprocessing is a therapy that was developed in the 1980s to help patients struggling with PTSD. It helps the brain process traumatic experiences that were overwhelming when they originally happened.

road ahead. I was certainly suffering from clinical depression. But this was more than that. The word for what I was feeling is *despair*.

Despair is a sickness of the soul that afflicts us when hope has totally disappeared. It's a lie that sneaks in and tells us that every day will be like today. It tells us there are no possibilities for a different future. We can endure a lot as human beings. But despair is a killer.

On a Tuesday in October of my senior year in college, after years of growing despair, I woke up and asked myself the questions I had asked most mornings during those years—is it still there? Is the cloud still there? Is there still a black hole within? Has anything happened overnight to help me feel human again?

The answers were the same as they had been, although with growing intensity, but for some reason that day was the day I decided I couldn't keep going like this. I still don't entirely know why the day went the way it did. I know a lot of people have come to a day like that and it's gone differently, sometimes with tragic results.

I felt myself go into a kind of autopilot. I grabbed a bag and packed it with some clothes with no conscious sense of why. I walked to my truck in student parking and sat in it while I tried to call a few people to see if they could help. But of course they couldn't. What I was facing couldn't be solved with a kind word.

I remember putting my truck in drive. The next thing I remember is pulling into the parking lot of a mental health hospital in town. I walked into the lobby and totally, completely fell apart.

———

This is something I know in my bones: Our strategies for holding things together are often the very things keeping us from being put back together. I believe this at every level, from the personal to the social to the global. The effect of Jesus' first blessings that I have seen in so many lives, including my own, is that they become guiding companions to accompany us into the dark interiors that we are terrified of visiting because we'll have to stop holding things together if we're going to go there. They teach us to abide the experience of that journey so that the demons that lurk there can be made into friends. Along the way, our fearful grip on the status quo is loosened, and hope begins to grow when we discover God meeting us there alongside our demons, our fears, our pain, our loss, our ache.

———

I admitted myself to the hospital and stayed there for days. I wept for hours and hours in a place that didn't give me any reason to hold anything together anymore. To be honest, the therapy work in the hospital wasn't that helpful. Some of the doctors seemed more depressed than the patients. Toward the end of my stay when I was feeling much, much better, a

LOL!
For
REAL!

121

very sad doctor checked in and asked if I was feeling suicidal, and it took all my restraint to not say, "No, but are you?"

Something happened there, though. It was more than psychological, although I think the healing experience included some long-delayed grieving that had been lodged in me for years, and there's plenty of psychology involved with that. Somehow my relationship to the poverty within, to the sense of loss, to the powerlessness, to the aching... it all changed.

Those feelings didn't so much go away as much as they lost their teeth. I had been longing for years for that fullness Paul talks about in Ephesians. It was the thing I had been seeking when I prayed that prayer back in high school at the conference. I had assumed, I think, that finding God within would mean these other things would disappear. That my wounds would be displaced by God. That my relationship to the world around me would change when that happened, too.

Instead, I discovered God lurking in the emptiness in a way that doesn't make it go away. And meeting God in that black hole inside has begun to help me find God in the craters left in the world by our violence.

I know a stay in a psychiatric facility may not sound like a monastic experience. There were no sacred icons on the walls. No brothers chanting the psalms. But I revere that hospital with the same sacred feeling I have when I think of the abbey overseas.

These are both places where I have discovered how the world within us and the world around us are so deeply connected, how the mystery of God meets us in both places, and how the hope we might look for in a change of circumstances actually comes to us in the last places we would ever look. It can be awfully hard to find God in the world beyond us when we haven't met God in the pain within us. But if we have, the encounter can dismantle the reactive energies we usually bring to the breaking points around us, which I suspect is the reason Jesus' blessings begin as words for the sufferers but then become words for the healers in the second half.

————

There's a line in the New Testament that captures this entire trajectory from the powerlessness we feel when the world breaks to the power we can find if we're willing to meet God in our inner world. It comes from a letter written by the apostle Paul to the Christians in the city of Rome. He's writing to people who face serious threats. The way of life they've discovered together is one that stands in stark contrast to the way things are around them. They're facing all kinds of attacks.

Paul isn't naïve about the things they're facing. He's been attacked in his own life, too. His awakening has cost him everything. Once he realized that the way to be faithful to Jesus was to give all his energies to the establishment of a new kind of human community where everyone belonged to everyone, he found himself targeted by all the powers and systems that were invested in teaching us to fear one another.

So in writing a letter of encouragement and exhortation to these Christians in Rome, he distills the thing he seems to have learned from his own experience. He tells them, "We boast in the hope of the glory of God. Not only so, but we also glory in our sufferings, because we know that suffering produces perseverance; perseverance, character; and character, hope. And hope does not put us to shame, because God's love has been poured out into our hearts through the Holy Spirit, who has been given to us."*

He sees a movement from suffering to perseverance, from perseverance to character, and from character to hope. So does Jesus.

The first blessings come alongside us and coax us into a reckoning with our suffering. It's not that Jesus is sadistic. He doesn't delight in our pain. But he loves us enough to tell us the truth about it—there's no way forward without facing it.

And Jesus knows that if we actually face our inner experience of suffering—the world he describes as poor in spirit, mourning, meek, and hungering and thirsting for righteousness—we'll find that rather than being swallowed up in a black hole of endless darkness, there's a bedrock of reality underneath those dark depths we avoid. This bedrock that he calls the kingdom of heaven can sustain us, but only if we consent to the journey into our pain that we so often avoid. If we consent, we will be formed in a whole new way. Our strategies for avoidance,

* Romans 5:2–5.

124

deflection, defense, and projection will be replaced with pos- tures of bravery and generosity, or as Paul calls it, character. And in the transformation of our character, we will find a hope that stretches itself out into our lives as we become true agents of the very transformation we long for.

This is a vision of hope that begins not as an attitude. Not as a faith commitment. Not as grit. It begins as a relationship with the Reality we connect to when we face our suffering. And then, as we are expanded to become the kind of people who are reconciled to everything within us and can therefore help put things back together around us, hope becomes a way of being in the world.

———

If you've made it this far with me, I hope you'll stick around. We're turning the corner now from the blessings that teach us to face our suffering, to the ones that speak new possibilities about a way of moving forward. It turns out the mysteries Jesus is pointing to and the hope they bring is felt not just in any particular Beatitude but in the arc of the whole piece. The hope is in discovering that the same sad, suffering, brokenhearted people he's speaking to at the beginning can become the kind of wounded healers that put the world back together. And you're about to see what I mean.

7

WE'RE NEVER MORE SURE OF OUR RIGHTEOUSNESS THAN WHEN WE KNOW THAT WE'VE BEEN WRONGED

Blessed are the merciful,
for they will be shown mercy.

A few years ago I was in Kenya working with a group of young leaders from around the world. They all came from places where things have broken in big and violent ways, where suffering and conflict and injustice have been widespread and seemingly continuous. Each delegate was doing some sort of work to help young people in their homeland resist patterns of violence and oppression and build new movements of healing and reconciliation. This wasn't a Christian gathering—among the delegates were people of pretty much every world faith—but I had the privilege of serving as a sort of chaplain, tending to the spiritual needs of these young leaders. I also facilitated some conversations around strategies for building and sustaining their movements and the big ideas that would help them do their best work.

One of the experts who brought one of those big ideas was a scholar from Harvard's Kennedy School of Government named Erica Chenoweth. Dr. Chenoweth's research focuses on political violence and its alternatives in pursuit of social change. If you're wondering about the best way to actually get what you want when it comes to sustained improvements in a broken world, Dr. Chenoweth might be the most preeminent scholar to learn from right now.

Dr. Chenoweth and a colleague coauthored a book called *Why Civil Resistance Works*. To write the book, they looked at every major movement seeking governmental change in the twentieth century, cataloguing whether these movements were violent or nonviolent. Their results emphatically demonstrated that nonviolent movements are better at getting what they want, and they explored the reasons why that's the case.*

The research in *Why Civil Resistance Works* focuses specifically on regime change, and I know the reason you picked up this book may not have been that you were looking to overthrow a corrupt government. You're looking for healing in your marriage. Or you don't know what to do with the diagnosis you just received. Maybe you're trying to figure out how to put things back together in a broken family or a hurting neighborhood. Or the headlines from national news have you burying your head in the sand because you just can't take any more of this. But it's possible, isn't it, that this research around nonviolent movements is pointing at something deep and universal? If the questions you're asking sound something like "How do I help make things better in a broken world?" then you're on common ground with Dr. Chenoweth.

On one of our nights together in Kenya, with a big bonfire in front of us and the delegates all gathered around it, I hosted a chat with Dr. Chenoweth to talk about this. We explored the soft edges that surround the hard data on political movements. The possibility that this research is naming something more

* If you want a good introduction to Dr. Chenoweth's work, check out their conversation with Ezra Klein on the *Vox Conversations* podcast from January 2, 2020.

widely applicable than the specifics of regime change. The conviction that violence is fundamentally the wrong tool to create peace. The hope that comes with the discovery that doing the work of putting the world back together in a nonviolent way isn't naïve. It's actually wise.

Broken worlds tend to stir up fervent moral commitments. THINGS SHOULDN'T BE THIS WAY. The panic that ensues—the existential urgency we feel to address the harm caused by bad actors—can leave us desperate to purge the evil from our midst, but if we're not careful, this purity impulse can be used to justify the worst kinds of violence in the name of righteousness. A deep ache opens up in the soul when we feel that the only way to hold things together is to violate our truest instincts on how things are meant to be.

How do we sift our own vengeful energies that rise up in us when a response to injustice is demanded?

This is an active question for those young leaders. It's an active question for us, too. I'm not just talking about the big social issues. And I'm not just talking about physical violence. I'm talking about the violent postures, the violent energies we bring to the world when it breaks. I'm talking about all the ways that vengeance cloaks itself in the guise of justice while doing more harm than good.

This is about neighborhoods where small infractions have led to deep grudges. It's about marriages where partners have felt betrayed. It's about national politics in the US and anywhere else where the stakes are high and the standards are impossibly low. It's even about our relationship with ourselves, because so many of us struggle to have compassion on ourselves and instead live in a kind of violent opposition to our own lives, our own souls. It can feel that we are our own worst traitors. Wherever we find a history of wrongs to be addressed, and enemies to be thwarted, we're dealing with the same fundamental questions Dr. Chenoweth is addressing. When the work reveals that we have to transcend the energies that have harmed us, we're talking about something universal. We're talking about *mercy.*

As we shared that conversation around the fire in Kenya, the feeling that a perennial mystery was greeting us in particular and concrete form was almost palpable. Something that transcends the specific context of political violence. However, I wondered how these young leaders could sustain a nonviolent posture in the world when they and their communities have suffered so much.

Dr. Chenoweth's work focuses on major social movements, but I've seen this posture and felt its power up close, too.

On my first trip to Israel/Palestine, I met a South African woman named Robi Damelin. Robi had been active in the anti-apartheid movement in South Africa before she moved to Israel in 1967 to get away from the pressure and ugliness of what was going on there.*

---

* You can learn more about Robi's story and work at https://www.theparentscircle .org/en/stories/robi-damelin_eng/.

We met with her to hear the story of her son David. Like all young Israeli Jewish men, he was required to enter military service when he turned eighteen. He had resisted the idea because of his concerns about the treatment of Palestinians under occupation. This is a question most of us have to ask from time to time: When should we try to do some good within a broken system, and when should we try to find a way to opt out of it? Ultimately he decided he would use the opportunity to demonstrate respect for the Palestinians while in uniform. After serving his required time, he was called back for reserve duty. He wrestled with those tensions all over again. While working at a security checkpoint during that second tour of duty, he was killed by a Palestinian sniper.

Robi learned of David's death from officers who came to her door to deliver the news. The first time I heard Robi tell this story, I remember her getting to this moment in it and wondering what it would be like to lose someone you love as much as a mother loves her son, and to lose them in such a horrific way. I remember trying to imagine what my response would be.

Tears?

Rage?

Denial?

Silence?

Breaking moments unleash an energy into the world, and it's usually not good. The pain they bring tends to bounce around the world like a pinball, gaining more energy with everything it hits. This is how small patterns of suffering can lead to greater patterns of suffering if we don't figure out how to break the cycle.

It's not as easy as simply pretending to not be hurting or angry, though, because we can't simply contain that energy. Even if we're resolved in our refusal to return that violence to the world, it will still find a way to do damage, either to us or others. This is why Richard Rohr says, "If we do not transform our pain, we will most assuredly transmit it."* One of the ways we often avoid the transformation of our pain is to deny it exists in the first place. That's why those first few blessings are so important. Jesus isn't asking us to pretend we aren't suffering. He's helping us face our suffering, which is an entirely different thing.

We were meeting with Robi because she has become a fierce advocate for transformation of the conflict between Israelis and Palestinians. She's no shrinking violet. She tells the truth about what happened, about what continues to happen in the conflict between Israelis and Palestinians. She's plainspoken about her suffering and the suffering of others.

However, when Robi heard the news from those officers, her response was different from anything I imagined. She immediately told them, "You may not kill anybody in the name of my child."

When I first heard that, a mix of feelings came. I was grateful for this little glimmer of hope because there's no way our world stops breaking if we keep insisting on an eye for an eye.

---

*Richard Rohr, *A Spring Within Us: A Book of Daily Meditations*.

I also felt a combination of awe and confoundedness. It's easy to say this is a brave, beautiful response, but it's also fair to say that it's strange.

Vengeance so easily cloaks itself in the guise of justice that we often don't know the difference, but the energy that drives vengeance is dark. It makes us small. And we easily become small and darkened when we suffer.

Robi had a different impulse that day. It was the kind of impulse that lives out the wisdom that Dr. Chenoweth shared with us in Kenya. She did something expansive and bright in a very dark moment. I've spent a long time wondering about how more of us could more often live like that, because it's pretty clear that if we don't, we'll keep breaking the world and breaking one another.

———

But how do we sustain that posture?

Like I explored in the last chapter, after blessing people in the most disempowering experiences, Jesus begins to speak blessings for people who have some power. He begins to speak to our agency.

The first blessing he gives in this new mode is for "the merciful, for they will be shown mercy."

If you're paying attention, you'll probably notice that a shift has occurred as we move through these blessings. To speak to those impoverished by their suffering, to speak to the empty-hearted and the empty-handed, is to speak to people who have been victimized. But to speak to the merciful is to speak to people who presumably have some options in their treatment of others. Mercy doesn't make sense as a category or character trait unless people are in the position to decide whether to show mercy in the first place.

What does Jesus even mean by *merciful*? The word in its original language has a range of possible meanings, including generosity to those with material needs. But another way of understanding it is to say that the merciful are those who "restrain [their] power over [someone else]."* In this sense, it describes someone with every right to demand revenge, but who decides not to exact it.

I keep discovering that when we suffer, we usually have to decide how to deal with the instinct that tells us we might need to hit back to make ourselves whole. When Robi lost her son, there was clearly a person responsible for his loss, and his death was a singular moment in a larger factional conflict that could have been used as a justification for unleashing a lot of violence against anyone on the other side.

This is where the mystery of this Beatitude begins to show itself, where the craft of paradox that Jesus keeps employing really does its work. When he blesses the merciful, my inclination is to think about all of the magnanimous moments in my life when I took the high road, to revel in the fact that finally,

* Eklund, *The Beatitudes through the Ages,* pg. 171.

Jesus is speaking to my pride. After calling me to face so much pain and misery, he's finally turned his attention to my virtue. He's bringing to mind all the grace I've shown, all the generous gifts I've given to other people in their need.

It's almost like misdirection. Like he *knows* those first few words will stir up my ego. It's like he's speaking to the part of me that wants to set myself apart from the unrighteous ones.

But then the second half of the blessing hits, and now that he's drawn my ego out into the open, out from hiding, he confronts it by offering a reward that I can only embrace if I recognize that I'm in need of mercy, too. The reward for the merciful is mercy. The whole thing is a setup.

Because of course, if Jesus wants to help us put the world back together, the one thing he can't do is feed the beast in me that wants to understand myself in opposition or superiority to others, to feel a feeling of self-ness that comes from me not being like them.

This raises plenty of questions. Will God really withhold grace from those who don't show it? And if it's really, truly mercy, then how does it maintain its un-deservedness if we earn it by offering it to others? But I've been more curious by what these blessings *do* in us lately. And this one has become a tethering force for me when I spin out in hurt and self-pity.

We're never more certain of our own righteousness than when we know that we've been wronged. But it can be terribly difficult to sift vengeance from justice when we're fixated on our own righteousness in opposition to those we stand against.

———

It's become common to speak of forgiveness in self-interested terms. We forgive and then discover that we're the ones who are set free. We forgive because to live in resentment is like drinking poison and hoping the other person dies. This is all true and helpful. If you're the victim of some abuse or offense, then pastors and therapists and other voices of wisdom should do whatever they can to help you no longer be held prisoner by what the abuser did, and it turns out forgiveness is part of that liberation for the victim.

However, as far as I can tell, this just isn't how Jesus and the writers of the New Testament speak of forgiveness. That doesn't mean it's wrong. But it's a different line of reasoning than the one Jesus uses.

Instructions on mercy and forgiveness are littered through Jesus' teachings and the early writings of the communities that followed him. It's part of the prayer he teaches us to pray.* But see if you notice the consistent logic in these teachings:

"Pray then in this way... forgive us our debts, as we also have forgiven our debtors... for if you forgive others their trespasses, your Heavenly Father will also forgive you."†

———

* In fact, in Matthew's version of the prayer, he offers commentary on the prayer immediately after he delivers it, and the one line he comments on is this one. It seems really important to Jesus that we get this.

† This is from the Lord's prayer in Matthew 6.

"Be kind to one another, tenderhearted, forgiving one another, as God in Christ has forgiven you." *

Pretty much every time it comes up, the teaching to forgive is built on the idea that we share with our offenders a dependence on mercy. The logic of forgiveness, of generously extending mercy to someone, is that we're fundamentally in the same boat with the people over whom we stand in judgment.

———

Now, this is dicey. This big idea—that we're all in need of mercy, that we share in common with everyone a need for divine generosity—has been used in terrible, abusive ways. It's been used to protect people in power at the expense of justice. It's been used to create false equivalencies between inequivalent wrongs. It's been used to stifle accountability. It's been used to perpetuate broken structures and to silence people. It's been used to gaslight victims and suggest that they're the ones causing harm by telling the truth.

I'm guessing this is one of the reasons that so much of our current discourse around mercy and forgiveness centers on the therapeutic benefits of forgiveness for the victim rather than the common need for mercy that unites all of us.

But when something true has been coopted by something

* Ephesians 4:32.

untrue, to prop up something that's broken, we shouldn't abdicate that truth and leave it in the hands of people who are using it in broken ways. We should wrestle it back, claim it again, reassert it apart from its abuse.

There's a fundamental difference between pursuing justice while remembering the humanity you share in common with the people you hold to account, and losing sight of that common need for mercy that makes us kindred with everyone. The idea that we could build a better world while dehumanizing the people whose power or sin stands opposed to that world is still an attempt to build a better world by forgetting the humanity of some within it, which is to commit the fundamental error of trying to solve a problem at the same level of thinking that created it.

When I read Jesus in the gospels, I don't see someone who's naïve about power dynamics and abusive structures. But he still makes this move and speaks to us about our common ground with the people over whom we hold the power of revenge.

This makes sense—if mercy will help us put the world back together, it has to lead us toward common ground. Any act of mercy whose underlying energy or motivation isn't unitive will fail to heal the divides.

This isn't about creating equivalencies. The fact that we're all offenders in need of grace does not mean that all offenses are equal. This isn't about silencing the truth or rejecting accountability. It's about the energy that drives our acts of truth-telling and accountability. People who show mercy because they know

they need mercy can do the work of justice while genuinely
wanting the healing of those who commit unjust acts.

———

Let me see if I can bring this down to the ground floor of our
lives with a couple of everyday stories, because it can be hard to
hold the thread between the big systemic stuff and the everyday breaking points we face.

First, an experience of my own. A few years ago, a story got told
about me that wasn't true. Some basic facts had a couple of layers
of misinterpretation and a few flat-out untruths added to them,
and it left me feeling hurt and unsafe. I found out this story was
being told about me because I started hearing about it from other
people. The story involved another person, and I freaked out and
shut down on them. I felt like they had twisted some details and
that any attempt to reengage them to set the record straight ran
the risk that they would just fold that new encounter into their
version of events. I know...you may be reading this and seeing
how my paranoia was part of the problem, and you may be right.

I nursed a lot of hurt around that whole experience. Some
of my closest friends were tied into it. It affected my work.
One day I was talking to a friend about the situation who was
familiar with the whole story. I was feeling indignant, looking
for someone to reinforce my feelings of self-righteous victimhood. I asked him if he thought I had done anything wrong.
I was really hoping for a clear, unequivocal "Nope. I saw it all

and you're clearly in the right. I'm sorry this person did this. You're innocent and good, and what they did is awful."

I think I believed that if someone would just say that to me, I could finally get on with showing some mercy. Once vindicated in my victimhood, I could finally get on with a magnanimous showing of grace.

But that's not what happened. I asked him about it, about whether I was missing something where I had done something wrong, and he said "Yeah."

I braced myself. He continued.

"You should have confronted the situation rather than going AWOL on it. When you realized that in their mind something was going on that wasn't, and that they were telling people this story, you should have reached out and clarified."

At first I wanted to defend myself. I felt the other person had shown a pattern of misinterpreting me in strange ways. How could I trust that anything I did to engage with this person wouldn't be similarly misinterpreted and used against me? But after I sat for a second, I realized I probably had more to learn from this.

For some of us, most of the harm we cause in the world comes from our actions. But for others, most of the harm, most of the breaking we cause, comes from our inaction. This is a matter of personality and individual stories and the ways we were nurtured (or not) and different kinds of stances that different people have in the world. Another way of saying it goes back to the thing I was describing in chapter 2, about the cases we build around our vulnerable souls. Some of those cases are built out of stances of aggression, and some are built with the raw materials of withdrawal. We all have lists of wrongs we committed in action, and we all have lists of wrongs we've committed through inaction, but for most of us, one of those lists is longer than the other.

I'm the kind of person whose long list is made up of the things I've failed to do.

So when my friend told me he thought the one thing I should have done differently was to confront this person when I found out the story that was being told rather than shut them down, he named a pattern in my life that I already had seen. If I hadn't already seen it, I don't think I could have received it. But I had and I did. It was humbling. The effect of my friend's feedback was that it caused me to soften in my stance toward this person. I still have my perspective on everything that happened. But I'm also a little more in touch today with what I might have in common with them.

———

I heard another example of the posture made possible by this Beatitude from a preacher named Nadia Bolz-Weber. Nadia is a Lutheran pastor, author, and public figure with a reputation for her unorthodox interpretation of Christian faith. I'm not sure her reputation for heresy is fairly earned though, because one thing that makes her come across as such a radical is her fierce commitment to a concept Christians have always claimed to believe in: grace. To hear her speak or read her work is to encounter a clear example of what it looks like when someone takes this blessing seriously.

One of my favorite stories she tells of trying to live this out involves an interview she did with a notorious sinner named Lance Armstrong. It was for a public event called the Nantucket Project. Armstrong, you may remember, was a legendary cyclist. He won championships all over the world, including seven times in the Tour de France. Making him even more of a standout in the field was the fact that he continued to excel after a potentially fatal battle with cancer. Lance endured a severe fall from grace, though, when it was revealed that he had used performance-enhancing drugs for years in a sophisticated scheme involving himself and others on his team. He had been revered as an icon of athletic achievement, and the reverence made the revelations of his cheating hit even harder among a fanbase who felt not just disappointed but betrayed.

As Nadia tells the story, when it became known that she would be interviewing Lance for the Nantucket Project event, a lot of people pressured her to go hard on him. It seems there was some sense that she needed to extract a public reckoning from Lance in front of an audience. What's peculiar about this is that, as far as I understand it, no one in that audience had been directly affected by what he did. Unless I'm mistaken, the sponsors who had aligned their corporate brands with Lance weren't there. His former teammates or opponents weren't there. This wasn't a crowd of people who had suffered real harm from what Lance did. But still, in a demonstration of

WHEN THE WORLD BREAKS

our all-too-predictable desire to feel better than someone else, these people wanted Nadia to read Lance the riot act.

But Nadia has been a consistent preacher of radical grace. She's not the type to obscure the truth about powerful people who abuse their power. But she seems to have thoroughly ingested the same understanding of human nature that Jesus is working with in this blessing.

Nadia set out to reframe the conversation, to infuse it with the posture of mutual humility that she champions, and she did so brilliantly with her opening greeting. Herself a public figure who's been open about a personal history of substance abuse, she simply said to Lance, "So, I see from my notes that you took some drugs you weren't supposed to and then you lied about it? OMG. I did that shit SO MANY TIMES!"*

This is what it looks like to stand in a posture of mercy grounded in one's own need of the same. A blessing for the merciful sounds like a celebration of our virtue, but the only reward Jesus offers requires us to recognize our own need for grace.

―――――

Once you begin to look for it, this kind of stance shows up everywhere. It's almost never the headline in the factional fights we're facing. But if you look for it, you'll find it. Aleksandr Solzhenitsyn was a Russian philosopher and novelist who was

―――――

* Nadia Bolz-Weber. Twitter, September 14, 2018.

145

exiled in the 1970s because of his criticism of the Communist regime. In spite of his resistance against what he saw as a corrupt government and the bad actors within it, he insisted on seeing the humanity in everyone. This was challenged by people who wanted him to more militantly take a side against those bad actors, and he wrote in a book called the *Gulag Archipelago*:

> "If only it were all so simple! If only there were evil people somewhere insidiously committing evil deeds, and it were necessary only to separate them from the rest of us and destroy them. But the line dividing good and evil cuts through the heart of every human being. And who is willing to destroy a piece of his own heart?"

He seems to know what we so often forget—there's no future without all of us. This doesn't mean you shouldn't have good boundaries. This doesn't mean we shouldn't protest and protect ourselves. But it does mean that as long as we believe "those people are the problem" rather than remembering that we share in common a problem that those people are acting out right now, we'll likely keep breaking the world.

We are terrified that the act of mercy will surrender our power to be made whole. But if Dr. Chenoweth's work is to be trusted (and it is), and if this strange blessing from Jesus is to be believed (and it is), then the best way forward in the face of our suffering is to resist the breaking forces while remembering the humanity we share.

8

CYNICISM IS A LIAR

Blessed are the pure in heart,
for they will see God.

In the months after that moment in high school where my memories resurfaced and set me off on a long journey toward healing, I noticed a new pattern in the way I related to the world around me. It wasn't good. I would have visceral reactions to anyone who felt even slightly unsafe, and the reactions were way out of proportion to the scale of whatever I was dealing with. Sometimes it was someone who was just a little bit overbearing in their attitude toward me, or it might have been that their body language was a little bit aggressive. I would go into a full-blown fear response. Sometimes I had to disappear from social situations without being able to explain why. (This was different from my lifelong affinity for an Irish goodbye when quietly slipping out of a party.)

After a lot of therapy and healing work, that reaction eventually went away. I don't think I've felt anything like it in years. But in those moments, it's clear to me that I was taking the threat of situations from much earlier in my life and projecting it into situations that had nothing to do with what had happened to me. This wasn't a process I was conscious of at the time, of course. It was an instinctual reaction. Something that rose up in my body as a fear response. Something that seized me whether I chose it or not. It meant that I felt unsafe in situations where I was perfectly safe. It meant I was suspicious of people who had given me no actual reason to be suspicious. It meant I saw danger in people where there wasn't any. I was reacting to people in ways that had nothing to do with them.

If you've suffered trauma or learned about the experience from others who have, this isn't a surprising thing for me to tell you. It's a common experience for any of us who have unhealed wounds. It's an understandable way that our bodies and brains try to keep us safe in a world in which we've been unsafe in the past.

But what happens when we keep seeing threats in situations where we're perfectly safe? What happens when our reactions to one another have nothing to do with the people we're interacting with? What happens when we see shadows where there aren't any? And what about when we're not just talking about the traumas in our personal histories, but the threats we keep seeing in the headlines of a world that breaks?

———

I'm one of those suckers who cut the cable to save money only to end up spending more on an endless list of streaming subscriptions. Despite it not working out as a financial advantage, there's at least one remaining upside to not having cable: I don't have many chances to watch cable news. However, I know these networks command a lot of our collective attention, so when I happen to take in the programming on one of those channels, like when I'm in an office waiting room with

a TV, I'm curious to see what they're saying. Or more impor-
tantly, what they're showing.

A few years ago, I was on an airplane sitting in an aisle seat.
Each seat had a monitor in the seatback, and from my vantage
point I could see what people were watching a few rows ahead
of me on the opposite side of the aisle. At one point I looked up
and was totally gripped by what was on the screen.

Apparently in some city, an older man had been randomly,
brutally assaulted on the sidewalk, and a surveillance camera
near the scene had captured the whole thing. The victim walking along the sidewalk. An assailant coming from nowhere and
striking him with a blow that put him on the ground. Him
getting punched and kicked while he lay there. It was awful.
Cold-blooded. Evil.

This cable news network was repeatedly playing a ten- or
twenty-second clip of the surveillance footage showing the
most gut-wrenching parts of the attack, looping it over and
over and over again, while a smaller picture-in-picture frame
showed a talking head giving some kind of commentary that I
couldn't hear. This must have gone on for at least five minutes
while I watched. I eventually snapped out of the trance and
realized that I was fixated on something I didn't really need
to be paying attention to, and I started wondering what was
going on in the imagination of the passenger who was staring
at that screen.

What happens to us when we fixate on cherry-picked scenes
of violence? What happened to that passenger? Was the fearful

151

part of their brain lighting up? When they got off that plane a few hours later, what would be the effect in them from watching that random assault again and again? How does someone who meditates on something like that see the world?

———

Steven Pinker is a psychologist and linguist who wrote a book a few years ago called *The Better Angels of Our Nature: Why Violence Has Declined.* It's a big book with a lot of data making the case that our world has steadily grown safer and exploring how that has happened. When I first bought the book, I had it sitting out on a table in my house, and a few visitors who noticed it during that time all made the same skeptical comment when they saw it: "Violence has declined? What is this guy talking about?" They were apparently convinced that we were living in an especially dangerous time.

They're not alone. It doesn't take a lot of searching online to find piles of survey data showing that our perception of danger has increased over the years. We're more and more convinced that a violent assault is right around the corner. That our kids are unsafe. That our fate is precarious at best. But we're actually living in one of the safest eras of human history.* (That's

———

* Tragically, as I write this, trends are headed in a negative direction and violent crime is on the rise in the US and elsewhere. However, the larger point still stands: Over the last few decades, Americans and others have shown a troubling disconnection between our perception of danger and the reality of it.

the case that Pinker makes, and from what I can tell, most serious readers have found his argument convincing.) Every time someone offered a scoffing reaction when they saw Pinker's book in my home, a little microcosm of a larger cultural reality was on display. Perception and reality have been headed in two different directions for a while now.

It's easy to feel like we're more informed than ever. With cable news and smartphones and social media, we have access to a staggering amount of information about what's happening around the world, and more and more of that information comes to us in the form of images and videos. You might think that all this extra information is a good thing.

In some ways, it is. In particular, the experiences of marginalized people have become more visible to those of us who were ignorant of those experiences, and that's a necessary improvement if we're going to get serious about building a more just world. Some of us legitimately have more to fear than others in the world as it is right now. It's one thing to read or hear about police brutality, for example, and reading about it is better than not learning about it at all. But it's another thing to see it play out against the bodies of people of color. That's the kind of information that can lead us to grieve these losses, ache for justice, and exercise our power to build something better.

But we're also more *formed* than ever by the endless feed of images and videos coming at us, highlighting threats not just against those most vulnerable, but random incidents of violence and disorder that leave us feeling that there are threats everywhere. It's one thing to wake up to the things that are broken in the world. We need to wake up, especially when the people with the most power and influence are unaware of how people with less power and influence are being treated. But the images a lot of us are meditating on have less to do with genuine realities and more to do with media companies and algorithms putting random images and videos in front of us whose only purpose is to keep our attention, because our attention is the commodity they're selling to advertisers. And when we incessantly meditate on the dark things in our world, there are unintended consequences.

This isn't a chapter about cable news or social media, though. Those channels of influence are just the peculiar examples that we can point to in the world right now. In any era, with or without cable news or social media, the bigger question we're asking is about the consequences that come with seeing the world as a place that's darker and more God-forsaken than it really is. It's about the danger in becoming people who see danger where there isn't any, who see the world through cynical lenses and therefore don't see it clearly at all.

In 1948, long before cable news and social media, a South African anti-apartheid activist named Alan Paton released a novel called *Cry, the Beloved Country.* The book takes its title from a refrain he uses from time to time to interrupt the plot of the novel with moments of lament. One of those interruptions goes like this:

> "Cry, the beloved country, for the unborn child that is the inheritor of our fear. Let him not love the earth too deeply. Let him not laugh too gladly when the water runs through his fingers, nor stand too silent when the setting sun makes red the veld with fire. Let him not be too moved when the birds of his land are singing, nor give too much of his heart to a mountain or a valley. For fear will rob him of all if he gives too much."

I first read this book back when I was in middle school, and I remember all the way back then being struck by both the truth and tragedy of what Paton was saying. He describes a child surrounded by beautiful things, swimming in a world saturated with the things that speak not just to our senses but to our souls, things that lead us to love the world we inhabit. And he calls his readers to weep for that child, because he knows the child will inherit a fear that will rob him of that love.

How does fear rob that child?

Maybe it's because it gets in the way of him resting in all the beauty that surrounds him, like salt in the water that surrounds someone in the ocean dying of thirst. They're surrounded by an abundance but totally unable to make use of it. Fear can prevent us from taking in all the good we inhabit.

But maybe it goes further than that. What if fear doesn't

simply cut us off from the goodness around us, but rather leads us to destroy it? If I'm afraid of you, I'm going to feel justified in the defenses I build against you. Defenses can easily turn into offenses. The things we use to protect ourselves often end up being the very tools of violence we use against others. Before we know it, our fear leads us to become the kind of people who break the world further. The cycle goes on, again and again, and in our fear we become the people who rob the world of its beauty by taking a wrecking ball to it in the name of our own cynicism and self-protection.

This cycle plays itself out at every level. In marriages and families, an inability to realize that we're seeing someone else through the lens of our own wounds and fears rather than in the light of who they are leads us to wage war where there was no need of it. In neighborhoods and churches and other community structures, suspicion leads us to throw stones at each other rather than understand each other. This cynicism is one part of the evil at work when people groups are demonized. When immigrants or people of color or LGBTQ people or any other identity group is cast in a suspicious light, for example, it's not just that fear is at work. It's that fear becomes a pretext for violence. We justify our defensive postures and don't realize we're using our power against people who've done nothing wrong.

Fear will rob us all if we remain stuck in this cycle, but I've come to understand Jesus' next blessing as an invitation to leave that cycle behind.

———

Jesus blesses "the pure in heart, for they will see God." (I know—you were wondering when we were going to get to it.) As with most of these blessings, it's not immediately clear what those words mean.

Who are the pure in heart?

Are these people with good morals?

Does this have to do with some kind of sexual purity? (That's been a common line of interpretation in some historical settings.)

Is purity of heart something we can achieve, or something we participate in when the Holy Spirit does her work?

Is this a description of people in the afterlife, after they've gone through some kind of purification that's not available to us in this life?*

Another way to come at it might be to ask, What is it that corrupts a heart? What makes a heart impure?

And what does it mean to see God?

Is this the vision of prophets like Isaiah who seem to have had some kind of ecstatic dream?†

Is this a promise for people who will see God in heaven when they die?

———

* Thanks again to Rebekah Eklund for her book *The Beatitudes through the Ages*, for informing this survey of interpretations.
† Isaiah 6, for example.

Is God hiding from all of us whose hearts aren't pure, so that even if we saw things with perfect vision, we wouldn't see God because God isn't there to be seen?

Or is God right here in plain sight for anyone with eyes to see?

Like I've said throughout the book, I'm not trying to offer the definitive, authoritative explanation of these strange blessings. I'm not sure I would trust anyone who is. I'm trying to tell you what these words have done in me, what they keep doing in me, and how they keep meeting me when the world breaks.

There's a connection between the condition of our inner world and the way we see and interpret the world around us. Later in the gospel of Matthew, in the same sermon that Jesus begins with the Beatitudes, he talks about vision again: "Why do you look at the speck of sawdust in your brother's eye and pay no attention to the plank in your own eye? How can you say to your brother, 'Let me take the speck out of your eye,' when all the time there is a plank in your own eye? You hypocrite, first take the plank out of your own eye, and then you will see clearly to remove the speck from your brother's eye."*

This is a strange situation. Who would have a plank in their eye? How could you even walk around like that? But the absurdity is the point. It's a metaphor for the kind of thing that happens all the time, behavior that's common but so often ignored. Jesus is objective enough to see the absurdity for what

* Matthew 7:3–5.

it is, and so he crafts an absurd metaphor to drive home the point. Someone is walking around with a major unresolved issue in their own life. It's a big enough deal that other people probably notice it, too. Its scale is dramatic. Its impact is significant. But rather than dealing with their own issue, this person sees an issue in someone else, and the issue they see is a small echo of the issue they're dealing with. Until they deal with their own issue, *they won't see clearly and they can't be trusted to deal with other issues.*

This is a pretty good image for what psychologists call projection. Or to quote a proverb I've heard from a number of teachers over the years: We don't see things as they are; we see things as we are. This is about our condition affecting our ability to assess other conditions.

This goes back to that experience I was having in the wake of those traumatic childhood memories, and it shows up with all of us when the world breaks: We take on a wound or inherit a fear, whether from personal experience or the stories in the headlines, and we begin to see the world around us through the lens of that unhealed hurt. Someone who has been wounded by betrayal is more likely to suspect betrayal in other situations. Someone who has been abused by someone with power is more likely to be suspicious of anyone in power. And all of us who keep meditating on the incessant stream of images and videos curated to keep our attention by raising our fear are likely to be affected. The shadows we carry end up being the shadows we see, even when they're not really there.

There's good news, though, for anyone who wants to step out of this pattern. It begins with the work of the first blessings Jesus gave, and it hinges on whether we understand what Jesus means by the "pure in heart." What if the pure-heartedness that Jesus has in mind isn't the purity of an unscathed soul? What if he's not talking about pretending to not be human, to not have desires? What if he's not blessing people who live up to some moral or sexual standard? What if purity of heart describes an inner life where the kingdom of heaven has found a home through the permeable boundaries of an impoverished spirit? What if he's talking about an inner world where the dark shadows of grief have been illuminated by a fresh vision of glory? What if he's talking about the kind of person whose desperate grasping has been transformed into trusting receiving? What if he's talking about the kind of person who maintains a taste for real righteousness, for true justice, rather than craving and gorging on a counterfeit feast? In other words, what if he's talking about an inner world that has been reconciled to itself? This is the effect of the first blessings. They call us to face the inner experiences we run from. If we trust those blessings, we might recover the kind of healed, reunited inner life that makes a heart pure. If that's the case, then the work we welcome when we trust those early blessings is going to help us.

But here's even more good news: It can work the other way, too. Sometimes learning to see God—in the world, in our neighbors, and especially in our enemies—is part of how we put things back together. It's the pure in heart who see

God, but learning to see God can be our path back to a pure heart, too.

———

Read the Bible and you'll get the impression that the world is saturated with God, revealing God everywhere. When it comes to creation, we have texts like the ones I referenced in chapter 3, saying things like *"The heavens declare the glory of God."** Or a letter from the New Testament, where Paul says that *"since the creation of the world God's invisible qualities—his eternal power and divine nature—have been clearly seen, being understood from what has been made."*†

When it comes to humanity in particular, the text speaks even more explicitly about finding God among us. The first thing the Bible ever says about humanity shows up in the first chapter of Genesis. As God is creating everything, God decides to make men and women in God's own image. The text describes us as bearers of the Divine imprint. Despite what you may have heard, the Bible never revokes that assessment. It *complicates* it, because there are other things that are true of us, too. Beautiful and terrible things. But any serious attempt to view humans the way Scripture does has to start with the idea that to see each other is in some way to catch a glimpse of God.

---

* Psalm 19:1.
† Romans 1:20.

Our church has a handful of mantras that help us stay clear on what we're doing and how we do it. We went with mantras because we wanted them to work as portable prayers that we can carry with us in our life together and our individual lives, too. One of those mantras is *Everyone an Icon*, and it comes from the assertion in Genesis that we bear the image of God. It reminds us that people aren't projects to tackle or problems to solve. It helps us learn to see every human being as a gift. It calls us to take seriously questions of inclusion and justice.

Because these mantras are central to our church life, I've preached about them a lot over the years. Usually when I cover *Everyone an Icon*, I tell a story that happened when I was in high school, working at Barnes & Noble. It was a busy day in the cafe, so I had been pulled over from my usual duty in the books part of the store to help in the cafe and make drinks. I was at the espresso machine slinging lattes, and my friend Jenny was taking people's orders at the cash register.

Before I get to the action in the story, you need to know that Jenny was wonderful. Bright, kind, clear in her communication. Friendly and professional. She knew the menu. She knew how to help customers feel welcome without burdening them with too much conversation. She was literally the ideal of who you would want when you walk in craving an overpriced, over-sugared dessert pretending to be coffee.

However, a woman came in and did something that everyone who has ever worked a service industry job has seen too many times: She treated Jenny with utter contempt for absolutely no reason. It was a preemptive strike that had nothing to do with Jenny, and it continued for a while. She belittled Jenny. She sneered at her. She made up reasons to be offended when Jenny had done nothing other than offer exceptional service. If you've ever worn an apron or worked behind a counter, I know I don't have to say more for you to get the picture. And if you haven't, I don't know if there's anything I can say to help you understand just how often perfectly "decent" people who probably have a great reputation for kindness and character end up treating other human beings like dirt.

Whenever I tell this story in the sermon about *Everyone an Icon*, I call the woman who was treating Jenny so poorly "Snotty Lady," and I usually make a joke about how I was over at the espresso machine watching this abuse and trying to figure out how to get some of my snot into Snotty Lady's drink.*

The rest of the story from that day in the cafe goes like this: While Snotty Lady was treating Jenny like dirt, one of our managers came in on her break to get a drink for herself. Snotty Lady didn't realize anyone was behind her, seeing her bad behavior, but Manager Lady was taking it all in. She

---

* I didn't actually do that, of course. This is not an endorsement of such behavior. But don't act like you're not at least a little bit disappointed that I didn't go through with it.

was a great boss. Savvy. Fair-minded. And very protective of her employees. On that day, I watched her execute the perfect intervention in defense of Jenny's dignity. It was an act of prophetic performance art delivered in a few sentences, built on something she knew about Jenny that would turn Snotty Lady on her heels.

The moment came when Snotty Lady briefly paused her assault against Jenny, taking a breath before continuing the offensive. In that moment, Manager Lady spoke up over the shoulder of Snotty Lady, speaking to Jenny directly. "Jenny," she said. "I heard you got into Harvard. That's so impressive. Are you excited?" This happened to be true. It also led to an immediate, radical conversion from Snotty Lady. One second she was treating Jenny like trash. The next, it was "Oh, Harvard?! How wonderful! My girlfriend's daughter went to Harvard! You'll loooooooove it." The hypocrisy was staggering. Suddenly Snotty Lady discovered there was a human being in front of her.

I use that story in the sermon because it's a simple setup to ask some hard questions about all the ways we fail to see the Divine image in other people. It presses into issues like status, privilege, social location, prejudice, and elitism. It's a quick parable about how any of us can trample on the depth, complexity, and dignity of other people. It's also a story where, in the telling of it, I was caught doing the very thing I was preaching against.

———

My friend Dave pastors a church in Belfast, Northern Ireland, and he invited me to preach my *Everyone an Icon* sermon there a couple of years ago. By this point I had delivered it a few times at our church in South Bend and elsewhere, so I felt like I had it pretty well dialed in. I told the story about Snotty Lady, preached through most of the rest of the sermon, and was coming in for the conclusion when someone at the church raised their hand. It was a fairly intimate gathering, so it's not like I could ignore the person with their hand in the air. I also wasn't sure if this was a normal thing for them during service. But I really enjoy some genuine give-and-take between me and the people I'm talking to, so I paused, acknowledged him, and asked what he had to say. With no preface or explanation, he simply asked a question, but in four words he indicted what I had just done: "What about Snotty Lady?"

When I preach *Everyone an Icon*, in addition to telling this story, I usually talk about "othering"—all the ways we see ourselves sharing humanity with some people and not others. And I offer some litmus tests to help us think about where and when we do it. We might be othering other people when we:

Fail to imagine that there's a story behind who they are and how they show up.

Assume we have nothing we could learn from them.

Feel threatened by them when they've given us no reason for fear.

Assume the things they say or believe are intrinsically suspect because of their identity or social location.

Turn them into one-dimensional caricatures rather than three-dimensional people.

The irony of what I did in the story is that I othered Snotty Lady, of course. Telling a story like that is a classic example of trying to solve a problem at the same level of thinking that created it. I'm not saying it's not a useful story. But a better telling of it would both call out the abuse against Jenny and simultaneously consider the possibilities of what led Snotty Lady to behave so badly, and to find solidarity with her, too. The truly transformative move isn't to feel indignant toward Snotty Lady. The transformative move is to realize how easily we become like her. If you can see the problem in Snotty Lady's behavior and still see the image of God in her, too, you're on the right track. Snotty Lady tried to make Jenny into a one-dimensional prop in her life that day. And I did the exact same thing to her.

———

I've thought a lot about that moment in Belfast at Dave's church. I don't know what provoked the question for the guy who raised his hand. But I know Belfast is a place that has faced the hard breaking of violent sectarian conflict. It's a place where the games we play, sifting the world between saints and villains, dividing the world between our people and enemies, have had disastrous consequences.

It's also a place where religion has been conscripted into the fight.* And while I hope my sermon that Sunday in Belfast helped more than it harmed, it's made me think a lot about the difference between religion that helps us see God in one another, and religion that hinders that process. The very thing that's meant to help us discover God in the places where we least expect to find God—in our shadows and in our enemies—can be used to corrupt our hearts to the point that we're blind to the Divine and therefore more capable of committing violence against It.

When Jesus blesses the pure in heart and says they will see God, I think this is a more subversive and surprising promise than it might sound like, especially if he's talking to people—to all of us—in the wake of suffering. To send us on the hunt for God in the world is to take a stance in favor of the best kind of spirituality and to call us away from cynicism we bring to our assessments.

Toxic religion preaches the scarcity of God. The high priests conspire like a cartel, as if they could lock down the supply of

---

* I'm not an expert on The Troubles that plagued Northern Ireland, but from what I understand, it's not really fair to say people were fighting over religion, Protestants vs. Catholics. Rather, those religious identities were wrapped up inside political identities. Which, by the way, is a stern warning for all of us in the US or other places where religion and politics are being fused together in the bitter fight.

the Divine within their control. But Jesus preaches the rampant availability of God. He declares God's kingdom to be so radically available that it can transform our worst experiences of suffering. In fact, he doesn't just preach it. He embodies it. And the idea of such pervasive light was so offensive to our shadows that we killed him. Impure hearts reigned that day, and their collective act was so evil that the day turned dark at noon and stayed that way for hours.

———

This is the paradox of Christ and cross. In Matthew 16, Jesus asks his followers who others say that he is. He's asking his inner circle to report to him on the rumors among the crowds. He's checking in on the public perception of his own life and work. His disciples report back to him that "some say John the Baptist; others say Elijah; and still others, Jeremiah or one of the prophets." These are pretty strong affirmations. The crowds are associating Jesus with some of the holy people of their history.

But then Jesus asks his closest followers who they say he is. As you follow the text, you're moving from the distant crowds to the inner circle. And before you consider his inner circle's response, consider how this often goes.

I've known a few people who've worked in close proximity to the most renowned religious leaders of our time. And what I've noticed in listening to them is that when you go from the outer circle to the inner circle, you rarely remain the same in your assessment of the religious leader you're working with. Tragically, and far too often, the people who move from the outer circle to the inner circle discover that a lot of what the religious figure stood for was at best an act. I've also known a fair amount of people who, in gaining closer proximity to a well-known religious leader, have sincerely reported that their esteem for that leader only increased. Those stories need to be told more often, because they're true, but they don't make the headlines at a time where cynicism is rampant and a leader who's reportedly faithful is considered too good to be true. But the point I'm making is that the movement from the crowd to the close confidantes almost never leaves the assessment unaffected. So when Jesus asks his closest followers what *they* think of him, we ought to be paying close attention.

Peter speaks up, and he says that Jesus is the Christ, the messiah, the anointed one. This is a big upgrade in the assessment. It's one thing to say that Jesus resembles the prophets of their history. It's another thing to say that he's the king they've been waiting for. This is the most elevated category Peter and his friends would have to describe the life of God at work in the flesh of a person. This is Peter saying, essentially, "I see God in you."

Jesus' response is interesting. And Peter's response to Jesus' response is even more telling.

Jesus affirms Peter's evaluation of his identity, but then goes on to say that he would suffer and die at the hands of the elders, the chief priests, and the teachers of the law. Peter says, "Never!" Jesus rebukes Peter and says, "Get behind me, Satan!" If Jesus calls you Satan, you're having a bad day. *LOL!*

This is the paradox of Christ and cross. We should all take a minute to have some sympathy for Peter in this moment. None of us expects divinity to suffer. None of us expects Christ to end up on the cross. Jesus is doing something transformative in this moment. He knows that if he simply affirms Peter's assessment of his identity as the anointed one, he'll be complicit in the same old tired assumptions we keep bringing to the world that break the world. We assume that God is present in power and status. We never expect God to show up on a cross.

Deuteronomy 21:23 said that "anyone who is hung on a pole is under God's curse." To be messiah, anointed, is to be under God's blessing, which is theoretically incompatible with being under God's curse. But that's the assumption that God is disrupting when Christ ends up on a cross.

For Jesus to claim the identity of the anointed one and then surrender to the curse of the cross is a way of training our vision. If we can notice the Divine light in him when he heals the sick, and when he confronts the corrupt powers, and when he loves his friends so well, and then if we can keep our eyes fixed on that light while it's obscured in the darkness of his death, then we might begin to be the people whose hearts are made pure, and whose vision is enlightened enough to see God everywhere.

Killing him wasn't the end of that light, thank God. (More on that in a later chapter.) But it's a searing reminder that our vision can become so jaded, so cynical, so darkened, that we could look upon God in the incarnation and see an enemy. If we could do that with Jesus, surely we do it with one another. The crucifixion can be understood in a lot of ways, but one clear angle is that it showed our tragic, devastating capacity to see through the darkened lenses of cynicism and kill the one who was God. And this blessing invites us out of that terrible pattern and into the healing of our vision.

———

This isn't a blessing for heads in the sand. This isn't a call to become naïve. If that's what Jesus was doing, he wouldn't have begun his teaching by blessing the poor in spirit or those aching for justice. Nothing good can come when we ignore suffering, whether our own or that of others. Denial is a weapon of evil.

But we have to go *further*. If we're going to open our eyes and take a look at reality, we need to see *more* of it, not less. If all we see is a broken world, we will perpetuate its brokenness. If we can't see God in our own lives, in our neighbors and enemies, and in the world at large, it'll be far too easy to commit harm. And those harms rise to the level of desecration, because they're committed against the image of God.

9

BELONGING IS THE PROBLEM UNTIL YOU KNOW YOU BELONG TO GOD

Blessed are the peacemakers,
for they will be called children of God.

Osheta Moore is a pastor and teacher who helps people do the work of putting things back together in a broken world by taking seriously the teachings of Jesus. A lot of that work focuses on racial justice. She wrote a book called *Dear White Peacemakers*, and if you haven't read it, you should put this book down and go read that one right now.

In the preface to the book, she tells the story of meeting with a coach at her son's school, along with the principal and his homeroom teacher, too. The coach had called her son the N-word. She tried to explain how hard it had been for their son when they moved to the area, and how his use of the slur had made her son feel unsafe. The coach denied it. Defended himself. Demurred.

Osheta talks about how others wanted her to go for blood. To push for a public reckoning with this coach. To demand his termination. And how she "was going to try to love the coach who called [her] son a horrific word." She wrestles with complicated questions in her own response. She faces the disappointment of others who think she should be more strident in her approach. She wonders if she's naïve. She talks about her desire to seek shalom—peace—and healing when she faces conflict. How she's only looking for love.

If you really start to see God in wider circles—circles that include even your enemies—you're going to need the next blessing, too. The path will cost you in ways you may not expect, but it's on the other side of those costs that a deeper reward is waiting.

Jesus blesses "the peacemakers, for they will be called children of God."*

The peacemakers.

Not the peace*keepers*.

The peacemakers.

This isn't a blessing for us when we're holding things together in a broken status quo. Like I said earlier, sometimes our strategies for holding things together are the very things that keep us from putting things back together. The difference between peacekeeping and peacemaking is a good example of what I mean.

Peacekeeping usually looks like the careful avoidance of any disruption to the current arrangement. Peacekeeping happens in marriages where conflict is never addressed. It happens in families where everyone pretends that Mom or Dad isn't an alcoholic. It happens when we keep acting as if our mental health isn't in the gutter because asking for help feels like the moment when everything might unravel. It happens when we walk into church or show up with our friends with a brave face in the form of a fake smile while everything is falling apart, because who wants to be the downer at the party?

___

* Matthew 5:9.

176

Peacekeeping happens when we tell people who are suffering in a system that's been built against them to stay silent, to pretend that everything is equitable and fine. It's the euphemism we use to describe troops who are deployed to threaten violence as a way of maintaining a situation that isn't peaceful for the people who endure it every day.

It turns out, of course, that peacekeeping isn't really the word for it though, because this isn't peace. Peace is a word for deep harmony and proper relationship. The New Testament understands peace as something God was doing through the life, death, and resurrection of Jesus, and it doesn't take too much reading in the gospels to discover that Jesus wasn't known for quietly accepting a broken status quo. Everywhere you look in these stories, you see him asking people to wake up and see the current arrangement for what it is. He asks a sick man, "Do you want to get well?" as if to stir up the man's latent discontent.* He walks into the temple and sees a system of exploitation at work in the complicated economics of temple taxes and sacrifices† and decides to flip the tables of the money changers and drive out the merchants with a whip. The "peace" we often keep is just a stable but broken status quo. If the situation isn't one of deep harmony and proper relationship, whatever it is we're keeping, it isn't peace.

However, if avoiding disruption isn't the same thing as

---

* John 5.
† Matthew 21, Mark 11, Luke 19, and John 2.

peacemaking, then choosing to disrupt isn't always peace-making, either. Sometimes we see a broken status quo and in our pain decide to wage war against anything or anyone that represents the world that has hurt us or others somehow. If peacekeeping isn't the same thing as peacemaking, then we should point out that not all acts of disruption are rooted in peace, either. Some acts of disruption and confrontation are just contemptuous fits of rage. Some of us are addicted to con-troversy. We don't know how to feel useful if we're not flipping tables. Our personal issues are parading as noble postures but the work isn't rooted in peace, especially when those acts of disruption continue to divide the world between the righteous and the unrighteous, perpetuating the kind of thinking or consciousness that so often breaks the world. Let's talk about that kind of thinking.

———

Humans are deeply wired for group identity. It's a way we feel safe. This helps explain everything from the passion we have for our team on the field to the dark intensity of the liberal/conservative divide. One way of understanding how we devel-oped this way goes back to the early days of our species, living in a setting where our physical safety was largely dependent on sticking with our people. To not belong was literally an exis-tential threat, and to be with our people was to be protected.

However it is that we ended up like this, this characteristic of humanity can be tested and observed, and when researchers have done that, they've found that we're even more susceptible to group identity than they expected.

The journalist Ezra Klein released a book a few years ago called *Why We're Polarized*, and I can't recommend it highly enough. No matter where you fall politically or theologically, it's an insightful read for anyone trying to understand our current divisions in the US (and with plenty of insights into human nature that apply anywhere). One of his chapters is called "Your Brain on Groups," and it surveys the things we've learned from the field of social psychology about why we're so prone to discrimination and us vs. them thinking. Henri Tajfel is one of the researchers whose work Klein draws on. Tajfel had a personal interest in studying group identity and discrimination: He was a Polish Jew who, when fighting in the French army in 1940, was captured and held as a prisoner of war by the Germans. He knew firsthand what it was like for a group identity to become a liability, and he saw the kind of devastation caused by these tendencies in human nature.

Tajfel had two hypotheses he wanted to test: "The first was that we were so tuned to sort the world into 'us' and 'them' that we would do so based on the lightest of cues. The second was that once we had sorted the world into 'us' and 'them,' we could act with favor toward our group and discriminate against the out-group—even in the absence of any reason to do so."* His experiments proved his hypotheses more dramatically than he imagined.

To set up the experiment, a group of teenage boys who all knew each other from the same school were brought in and asked to each estimate the number of dots in an image with too many dots to count one by one. They were told this was an experiment to test "visual judgment." Then the boys were asked to participate in another experiment, and they were told by the researchers this second exercise had nothing to do with the first. They were separated into two groups and asked to distribute cash to the other boys. The researchers told them that to make things easy, they would establish the two groups based on which boys in the first experiment underestimated the number of dots and which boys overestimated the number.

Imagine yourself in this situation. You're there with your classmates, and you've each just made a guess at the number of dots you were looking at. Then the researchers tell you you're a part of the "overestimating" group or the "underestimating" group. Then they give you cash and ask you to distribute it to other boys in either group. These groups are made up of your classmates. There are preexisting bonds among the group that have nothing to do with who overestimated or underestimated the number of dots. Do you think you'd be influenced by the flimsy group boundary created artificially by the researchers? These boys were. They showed favor in distributing cash to

---

* Ezra Klein, *Why We're Polarized*, pg. 52.

their fellow over-counters or under-counters and discrimination against the boys in the other group. This totally trivial group
distinction was enough to entice these boys into discriminatory behavior.

Tajfel and his team constructed other experiments to see if
the results would hold (they did), and they also introduced a
new layer. In one experiment, they offered different scenarios
for the groups to choose from in the distribution of money:
In scenario (A), your group would get more money than your
group would get in scenario (B), but in scenario (A) the other
group would also get more money. In scenario (B), your group
gets less money than it gets in scenario (A), but the other group
suffers more. The groups favored scenario (B). They were more
interested in having more than the other group than in simply
having more. This doesn't just demonstrate a need for group
belonging. It shows an instinctual need for our group to beat
other groups.

One reason we may be naïve about this group identity stuff
is that, in spite of the trivial stakes that inspired it in Tajfel's
experiments, much of the time we carry these group identities
and observe their boundaries in quiet or subtle ways. Whatever the
boundary is—political, racial, religious, ethnic, geographic—
when we feel especially safe, we may not even realize it's there.
That doesn't mean it isn't baked into the world we've built,
with prejudicial systems and problematic structures that maintain group supremacy whether we're aware of it or not. But
we don't feel as much need for belonging when we feel safe

because belonging is something we retreat to when we don't. I heard Klein in a podcast interview about his book summarize it like this: "Identity activates under threat."*

If you think about the way polarizing political rhetoric works, it's always fear based. Polarizing leaders tell their people that other people—other groups—are a threat to them, and that they, the leader, will protect them. We can try to step back and see this for how problematic it is, but we're all susceptible to it, too. The research is pretty clear that these tendencies are wired deeply in all of us. This is the level of consciousness that has to be subverted if we're going to put things back together.

———

There's a moment in the gospels where Jesus does something that has always intrigued me, and the more I've come to understand this research about human nature, the more I think he was dealing with this particular issue.

In the gospel of Luke, the first three chapters are the prelude. They tell the stories of Jesus' conception and birth, and they locate all that action in both the history of the Jewish people and the political context of the first century. When you read in those chapters about Jesus being presented at the temple, or the long list of his genealogy, that's the narrator's way of locating him in the history of the Jewish people. When you

———

* I wish I could remember what podcast I heard this on.

read in those chapters about the reign of Tiberius Caesar and how Pontius Pilate was governor of Judea, that's the narrator's way of locating him in the political context of the first century. It's also a reminder of what I said in the first chapter—Jesus lived in circumstances that were loaded with complications not unlike the world we're living in today.

If the first three chapters are prelude, that makes chapter four the inaugural moment in Jesus' ministry. It's not just one story from all the work he did. Like any inauguration, it sets a theme. You could say it's a story to teach all of us what's going to be required of us if we want to follow him.

In the story, Jesus has just returned from his temptation in the wilderness, which he entered after his baptism. (Hold on to that detail—it'll matter a little later here.) He returns to Galilee "in the power of the Spirit," comes to his hometown of Nazareth, and shows up at the synagogue on the Sabbath. He's handed a scroll of Scripture, and he reads from Isaiah a text that begins:

> *"The Spirit of the Lord is on me,*
> *because he has anointed me*
> *to proclaim good news to the poor."*

The Scripture he reads goes on to proclaim "the year of the Lord." There's a lot going on here. These texts are loaded with expectation for Jesus and his people. They come from centuries earlier, but they hold the hope of a future when God would raise someone up who would bring God's favor to the people. After Jesus finishes reading, he puts down the scroll, and he has the audacity to say, "Today this scripture is fulfilled in your hearing." He says he's the one through whom this promise will show up.

The people are thrilled. They speak well of him. They say to one another, "Isn't this Joseph's son?" In other words, hometown boy's gonna be the hero.

Then, just six verses later in the story, we read this: "All the people in the synagogue were furious…They got up, drove him out of the town, and took him to the brow of the hill on which the town was built, in order to throw him off the cliff."

What?

In verse 22, they're saying "Amen, preacher!" But by verse 28, they're saying "Kill the preacher!" What happened to transform the congregation from raving fans to a violent mob?

He betrayed their group boundary.

Between the moment when Jesus tells the people that God has anointed him to bring God's favor and the moment when the people try to kill him, he basically says "You're going to ask me to perform a miracle, but the only miracles you'll see are like the ones from the time of Elijah and Elisha…" and then he retells two stories from their people's history when Jewish prophets performed miracles for Gentiles. People from another group. Did you catch what happened here?

In the inaugural story of Jesus' ministry—the story that sets the theme—Jesus tells the people that God is here, doing the things God promised to do, but the activity of God is going to take place beyond the boundaries you've drawn between your group and everyone else.* And they absolutely cannot handle it. We have an instinctual need for our group to beat other groups. When that need is confronted, our group identity gets activated, and we have to purge the person who's threatening it.

———

Once you notice this theme, it stands out elsewhere in the gospels, too. Later in Luke, in chapter 10, Jesus is asked by a religious expert what's required in order to inherit eternal life. Jesus turns the question back on the expert, who sums it up by saying to love God and love your neighbor. Jesus agrees. Then the expert asks another question: "Who is my neighbor?"

This is a question we're constantly asking whether we realize it or not. It's with us in all our interpersonal conflict. It's with us when we do the othering that I talked about in the last chapter, assuming some people are suspicious when they've given us no real reason to fear. It's with us when we find ourselves having greater empathy for people who look like us than for people who don't. It's with us when we turn a blind eye to

———

* By the way, stories like this from the gospels have been used to fuel anti-Semitic ideas, painting the Jewish people as xenophobic. But the irony of using a story about Jesus pushing back against group prejudice to justify a group prejudice is staggering. This isn't a story for us to use to cast a group of people in a negative light. It's a story meant to dismantle that very impulse.

discriminatory systems. It's with us when we walk into the voting booth. At its heart, this question seeks a limiting principle on the law of love. It's as if the religious expert is asking Jesus to define just how wide the circle needs to be for him, and it assumes that once that boundary is drawn, he can ignore—or maybe even treat as an enemy—anyone who exists beyond it.

To respond, Jesus tells a story. You've probably heard it before.

He describes a man traveling the road from Jerusalem to Jericho, which was a dangerous road. He's attacked by robbers, stripped, and left for dead. Two different religious figures pass this man on the side of the road, noticing him but failing to intervene. Before we get to the next character who enters the story, we should consider for a moment what it means that they noticed him. What did they actually see?

Maybe they saw an inconvenience. Dealing with a man beaten and left for dead probably meant arriving late at their next destination. It might even cause them to shirk some professional responsibilities that were waiting for them at the end of their trip.

Or maybe they saw something more than an inconvenience. Maybe they saw a threat. This was a dangerous road, known to be stalked by gangs of robbers who lay in wait for victims. A man robbed and left for dead was as good as a sign posted that would have said: "There are threats nearby."

These are at least a couple of the ways we see each other without seeing each other. Ways that we implicitly decide that someone is outside the circle of our compassion. Beyond the limiting principle of the law of love. Jesus has created a situation that might have given those characters an out. But of course, if you keep listening, you'll see that he's not interested in giving us any kind of exemption on the law of love.

Next, a Samaritan enters the scene. This is a character from a different group. An outsider. Someone who was religiously and ethnically suspect—impure—in the eyes of the people Jesus was talking to. And it's the Samaritan who tends to the needs of the victim on the road.

Sometimes I like to play with this parable when I'm talking to people who are familiar with it. I'll ask them if they remember the setup that Jesus was responding to, and they'll say, "Jesus was talking about loving our neighbors, and someone asked him who is his neighbor."

Great, I'll say. Then I'll ask, what was Jesus' answer?

And sometimes, if I can get them to answer quickly enough, they'll respond, "The Samaritan."

But that's not Jesus' answer to the question "Who is my neighbor?" The trick with this parable is that Jesus essentially refuses to answer the question because *it's not a good question.* It's a question that assumes that a line can be drawn between the people I'm supposed to love and the people I can ignore or dehumanize.

I said above that Jesus "describes a man," but in fact he doesn't really describe the man at all. He doesn't offer any identifying characteristics. We don't know where this guy is from, whether he's rich or poor, whether he's a part of a political-religious faction like the Zealots or the Pharisees. The character in the parable that stands in as an answer to the expert's question is a non-answer. Jesus knows this guy is doing what all of us do: hoping we can divide the world between those we should love and everyone else. He essentially tells a story to dismantle the religious expert's question and replace it with a better one: *Will you be the one who loves?* And then, as the model citizen in the story Jesus tells, a Samaritan—an outsider—shows up.

It's as if anywhere Jesus senses a group boundary that's being used to keep some people in and others out, he challenges it.

This is a warning for all of us. Everyone wants to be on the home team. We're all carrying group identities within ourselves that we use to define ourselves. When we're feeling safe—or when our group is prospering more than other groups—these identities may be quiet, dormant, in the background of our lives. But when the favor extends to the outsiders who dwell beyond the boundary of our group, we'll be tempted by the same violence that the crowd demonstrated in the synagogue that day.

———

This is a problem for anyone who starts seeing God in wider circles, especially when those circles come to include people who belong to other groups. This means that this is going to be a problem for peacemakers because we have to subvert this groupishness if we're going to live with deep harmony and proper relationship.

It's so often this group identity stuff that breaks our world. It's clearly wreaking havoc right now. Putting things back together requires us to work against the weaponization of group identity. It calls us to walk out beyond the circled wagons into the no-man's-land between our people and everyone else.

I learned a good word for this territory when I was back in Belfast not long ago. My friend Jonny works with the same Corrymeela community I mentioned in chapter 6 when quoting Pádraig Ó Tuama. Every month Jonny convenes an evening gathering in a pub for music, activism, community, and reflection at the intersection of art, justice, reconciliation, and faith. These are meant to be nights of lament and healing for a place that has been absolutely devastated by the kind of violence I've been talking about here. Northern Ireland endured decades of factional conflict at the end of the last century, and there are still so many wounds there that remain unhealed. They call these monthly events "Borderlands." They're meant to nurture life in the liminal space between groups that have been at war with one another.

The Borderlands are a dangerous place. When you walk beyond the boundary of your own group toward others, you're going to be seen as an enemy by the people you're approaching. Even worse, your own people will brand you a traitor, and there may not be a category for which we have greater scorn than "traitor." This is what happened to Jesus in Luke 4. He wasn't threatened because he had the audacity to claim the title of "anointed" for himself. He was threatened because he had the bravery to suggest that God's work would happen beyond the boundary of their group.

I've met some legitimate peacemakers in my life. Some of them are members of our church, doing this kind of work right here in South Bend. I've also met them in the places I travel to, places I go to so I can learn how it is that we can put things back together again. And one of the ways I've heard them describe their experience again and again is this: It's *lonely.* Your own people shun you and every other group still doesn't trust you. And if you're really going to maintain this peacemaking posture in the world, even if the group you came from would have you back or the groups you're reaching out to would fold you in, you may have to resist those opportunities, because inclusion so often comes with strings attached, demanding your loyalty to the people in one group at the expense of your love for others. You have to maintain some kind of independence from all this groupish stuff if you're going to keep making peace. This is where the second half of the seventh blessing, where Jesus says the peacemakers will be called children of God, turns out to be so important.

———

Remember when I said the scene from Luke 4 with Jesus in the synagogue happened right after Jesus returned from his temptation in the wilderness, which he entered after his baptism? This is important for what we're talking about.

In Jesus' temptation in the wilderness, he's presented with three challenges. The devil confronts his hunger and tells him to cause stones to become bread; the devil offers Jesus all the kingdoms of the world if Jesus will bow down to him; and the devil brings him to the roof of the temple and tells him to throw himself down so that God will send angels to catch him. We could argue all day about what the Bible means by "the devil" and whether a guy with horns on his head was out there messing with Jesus. But there are more interesting things going on here, like the thread that's woven through all three temptations: The devil begins each challenge by saying, "If you are the son of God..."

Right before these temptations, Jesus was baptized in the Jordan River. When he came up out of the water, God spoke from heaven and said, "You are my son, whom I love; with you I am well pleased."* Everything that happens in Jesus' adult life and ministry, from the temptations in the wilderness to the teachings in the sermon on the mount, from healings and confrontations with power to his death and resurrection, is preceded by this experience: Jesus has a firsthand encounter with his belonging in God the Father.

Jesus was baptized not just in water but in Divine belonging. He knew something in that moment—in his spirit, in his body, in his mind, with every part of himself—that would sustain him in every other moment.

---

* Luke 4:22.

There is a kind of belonging that feels good but that plants the seeds of violence in all of us. It enters our experience at the reptilian base of the brain where things like fight or flight (or fawn) come from. It locks us in at one level of consciousness and resists any movement toward anything higher or better. It's the raw material from which prejudice comes. This kind of belonging must have tempted Jesus when the crowd at the synagogue cheered for him.

But there is another kind of belonging that we have access to.

Divine belonging doesn't get to you at the base of the brain stem. It emanates from a deeper place within. It's strengthened with every step we take into deeper communion with our own souls, since it's in that deep place within where we meet God. It's also on offer with every step we take into the Borderlands.

Like with some of these other blessings, I've come to believe you can access its promise from either end. We can be formed more and more deeply in our knowledge of our belonging with God. The practices of Christians through the centuries, at their best, have often been the kind of thing that helps this knowledge root itself more and more deeply in us. And from that knowledge we can find the strength to walk the sometimes lonely path of peace.

But it can also be that we find ourselves in the no-man's-land between the warring factions, taking friendly fire from behind and enemy fire from everyone ahead, where we are stripped bare of any group belonging, and then find ourselves baptized with a wave of the Spirit who speaks to us and tells us we belong to God.

The reward Jesus promises peacemakers is that they will be called children of God. As beautiful and heartwarming as that sounds, I've come to believe that the reason this is the reward Jesus promises peacemakers is that he knows *no one else will claim them.* If you really gain a vision for God in everyone, not just the people in your group; or if you begin to see how the world will keep breaking as long as we remain addicted to the kind of belonging with our own groups that causes us to see other groups as threats, you're probably going to end up in a wilderness not unlike the one Jesus faced. The group you left will see you as a traitor. The groups you're approaching will still see you as an enemy. But it's out there in that wilderness where you're given the chance to experience your belonging with God.

Those peacemakers I mentioned who talk about how lonely their work is—most of them will also tell you they wouldn't trade that work for the world. If you ask a follow-up question and try to understand why, and if you're waiting for an explanation that would satisfy the survival instincts that most of us are living by on most days, you may not be satisfied with what you hear. But if you listen at another frequency—not just the frequency of fear or ego or comfort, but the frequency of the soul—you may discover that they've found something we're all longing for. To be at home with God is to be at home anywhere.

So good!! Love that.

This is another one of those blessings that first sounds quaint, and then when further considered becomes troubling because it carries within it a knowledge of the difficulty we will face as we try to make peace, but that ultimately turns out to bless and honor at a level of depth and transcendence that shakes the soul.

10

EVIL IS A LIMITED RESOURCE

Blessed are those who are persecuted because
of righteousness,
    for theirs is the kingdom of heaven.

Now, at the end, we come to what might sound like a dark promise. If you simply stumble into these words, it may not feel like they offer much. But if you've allowed the other blessings to do their work, or if you simply keep your eyes open when the world breaks, you may discover that this is the most hopeful thing Jesus says. He blesses "those who are persecuted because of righteousness, for theirs is the kingdom of heaven." I want to show you how everything Jesus knows about life in a broken world is gathered up and named in this blessing, and how his own life demonstrates the power and hope of this knowledge.

First, we have to deal with the idea of persecution. Or more specifically, persecution on account of one's righteousness. That's an important qualifier.

In the culture wars of our current moment, it's easy for all of us to feel attacked. Left, right, conservative, liberal, Christian, atheist... everyone's a little on edge. A little too quick to read every slight as an attack. To cast oneself in the role of the martyr. It feels like everyone's convinced that the world has become especially hostile to them.

Christians in the West, accustomed to the centuries of cultural dominance we've enjoyed, are feeling especially tender about some of this stuff. I'm not saying there aren't genuine and important questions we're facing about how to create a society that has room for diverse, deeply held convictions. That's trickier than anyone seems to want to let on. But let's be clear: Jesus isn't talking about discomfort. He's not talking about being decentered. He's not talking about being offended. He's not talking about having your preferences relativized in order to make room for other people with different perspectives and experiences.

The root of the Greek word for *persecuted* here refers to being pursued, and the pursuit is instigated because of someone's righteousness. Because of their investment in justice. Jesus is talking about evil coming after you because you are a threat to its project. This is a blessing reserved for people who need to be taken out if evil will continue.

Throughout Scripture, evil takes on personified form, as if it has a will, as if its energies are directed with intent. This is often what it feels like when the world breaks. The way it wounds you—the way it *comes after you*—has the feeling of a personal vendetta. When you read in 1 Peter 5:8 that "your enemy the devil prowls around like a roaring lion looking for someone to devour," you're reading a letter that many scholars believe was written during the time when the Roman emperor was directing severe persecution against the Christians this letter was written for. This is a word for people whose way of being with one another was at odds with the ways of the empire. Somehow their life together became an act of resistance against it. And so evil came for them.

When we said earlier that whatever we are fighting cannot be defeated by the power that created it, we were talking about evil and the need to root our lives in something fundamentally different from its energies. But when we root our lives in a power unlike the power that breaks the world, we can assume that evil will come for us. After all, that's what happened to Jesus. Persecution threatened him throughout his life, like in the moment in Luke 4 when the synagogue crowd goes from "Amen, preacher!" to "Kill the preacher!" and tries to throw him off a cliff. And of course it ended his life when he was crucified.

It's those events—Jesus' death and everything that followed—that make sense of this blessing. But before we explore that, it's worth taking a step back and observing the way Jesus lived in the flow of the other strange blessings. If you watch his life, listen to the other things he says, and generally pay attention, you'll see someone who entrusted himself to the very picture of reality he was teaching us to trust.

———

When Jesus blesses the poor in spirit, knowing that we are conduits, not sources, it was because he had lived the kind of open-hearted, permeable-soul existence that he called us to. When challenged about the miracles he was performing in John 5, he said, "Very truly I tell you, the Son can do nothing by himself;

he can do only what he sees his Father doing, because whatever the Father does the Son also does."*

This is an expression of dependence coming from Jesus that a lot of us would be uncomfortable with if it were used to describe us. We would like to think of ourselves as self-sufficient sources, not empty vessels. But apparently Jesus embraced the emptiness within himself in a way that we resist, because one of the earliest hymns sung about him was the one I mentioned in the second chapter: "Christ, being in very nature God, did not consider equality with God something to be grasped, but rather he emptied himself."

When Jesus blesses those who mourn, I trust him because I see him more easily moved to tears and lament than I am most days. He weeps over Jerusalem because the city doesn't know the things that make for peace. He weeps for Lazarus who had just died, even though I suspect he knows he's about to raise him up. The writer of Hebrews says that "during the days of Jesus' life on earth, he offered up prayers and petitions with fervent cries and tears."†

Any version of a king that I would have expected would not have included this quick move toward weeping. Any vision of strength that comes natural to me is one without tears. But Jesus wasn't afraid to have his heart broken by a broken world.

When Jesus blesses the meek, I trust him because his

---

* John 5:19.
† Hebrews 5:7.

strength was so frequently bridled, either by his own character or by the circumstances around him. He was bound as a prisoner, beaten and whipped, and hung on a cross. A lot of people have said he surely could have come down from the cross, because our visions of God have more to do with our assumptions about God's invincibility than God's revealed capacity for vulnerability. But I don't know. What I see in Jesus is a man who knew that he would receive the life he needed, regardless of whether he could take it for himself.

When Jesus blesses those who hunger and thirst for righteousness, I trust him because I see him aching, groaning, for things to be right. I hear the screaming inside when he cries out on the cross, "My God, my God, why have you forsaken me?" Any of us in that moment would know the screaming inside, too, while suffering such personal injustice. But I also sense the desperation in his desire for justice when he flips tables in the temple, when his anger burns in the woes he speaks to the people most invested in an unjust system. He knows not just his own desire for justice, but the famine that plagues a whole world desperate for things to be put back together in an equitable way.

When Jesus speaks to the merciful and reminds them of their need for mercy, he does so as a man who had extended mercy without ever requiring it for himself. Surely he's authorized to ask us to do the same when we are so deeply in need.

When Jesus speaks to the pure in heart, he does so as a man who saw a woman for her devotion, not her reputation. He saw a tax collector—a traitor to his people—for his capacity for faithfulness. He saw a Roman centurion, the representative of the oppressors of his people, with the same subversive lens. Jesus was not naïve to the broken world he inhabited, but he might have been the least cynical person who ever lived. He seems to have seen God everywhere.

When Jesus speaks to the peacemakers, he does so knowing the alienation that comes for everyone who makes peace. Having heard his own belonging with the Father called out at his baptism, he walked the lonely road that calls all of us beyond the safe confines of the groups that demand our loyalty. He blesses the peacemakers knowing his death would somehow tear down walls of division and create the possibility of a new, universal human community. I know the Church has had plenty of chapters in its history that did not bring peace, but the early community of disciples that grew into the church became the place where it could credibly be said that every conceivable line of division—class, race, ethnicity, religion, gender—was being overcome in love. And those bonds of peace were somehow established in his own life and death.

———

But what about when he blesses the persecuted? Where's the hope in this? You find it when you take stock of everything that was revealed in the persecution Jesus suffered.

In the last hours of Jesus' life before he was crucified, you can see the gathered forces of evil in every expression. Evil brought everything it had against Jesus.

He was betrayed, not just by Judas, but by the others who followed him, too. His closest friends, the ones who had walked with him for years, who had experienced his inexhaustible generosity, who had seen the way he healed, who had rallied when he confronted the leaders of the various factions who saw him as a threat, who had known his love in the most compelling ways, turned him over or ran away. For many of us, the deepest breaking we've ever known has been in the betrayal of someone close to us. Infidelity. Deceit. Abandonment. These betrayals cast some of the darkest shadows.

But he didn't just endure the betrayal of his friends. Religion was used against him, too. They painted him as a threat to their identity as the faithful people of God. Claims of his blasphemies were a way of saying that he was an impurity that must be purged, while the people were oblivious to the fact that it was their own infidelities they projected onto him. The human impulse to make scapegoats of the innocent has led to some of our most vile acts in history, and this was one of those vile moments.

The power players among the political elites conspired that day as well. A complex status quo arranged between the empire and the people whose lands they occupied was held together by the threat of violence, and on days when it seemed the threat was not enough to maintain order, they had to follow through on those ugly promises. This was one of those days.

His own body was used against him. The beatings were only a precursor to the torture he would endure in his actual crucifixion—a method of execution designed with a sadistic intelligence by people who wanted to create the most extreme and extended public spectacle of suffering so that others would be deterred from threatening their power.

When Jesus describes persecution, it's not a theoretical experience. In his own life and death, you can see evil unloading its entire arsenal against him. Evil brings everything it has to the fight. And for three days, it looks like evil has the final word. It looks like violence has overcome his life. It looks like all his promises were naïve. It seems the bedrock picture of reality that he had described as the kingdom of heaven had only been a mirage, because its rewards were nowhere to be found when he hung on a cross and lay dead in a tomb.

———

But... that's not the end of the story. Now, I know a lot of people find the idea of Jesus' resurrection to be an absurd fantasy clung to by religious fanatics who have checked their brains at the door. We should talk about that for a minute.

This isn't a book written to argue with you about the resurrection or to try to talk you into any other claim of faith. I'm not sure those arguments ever really do much. But the way I've come to understand these blessings and the picture of reality they point to—or better yet, the way I'm learning to *trust* these blessings and the picture of reality they point to—is tied deeply to that event when, three days after evil had unloaded its entire arsenal on Jesus, he came out of the grave.

I could talk to you about first-century expectations and the similarities and differences between the gospel stories of Jesus' resurrection and other ancient mythologies involving heroes being brought back to life. We could explore things like the criterion of embarrassment or mutual attestation. These are thoughtful approaches that I think make a lot of sense when trying to evaluate the credibility of an ancient historical claim. It's good to give the brain something to chew on while the heart does its work. But rather than get into those technical areas, let me just offer this for the skeptics who have stuck with me this far. I know you may find yourself a little disappointed that in the end I'm going to hang the whole thing on a hook you fear can carry no weight. I get it. And I love that you're not willing to check your brain at the door. This may not get you any closer to seeing it the way I see it, but I'll explain it like this: Whatever happened after Jesus was crucified, that day two thousand years ago is at the epicenter of such a radical wave of personal and societal transformation that I honestly think anyone claiming a resurrection didn't happen has a heavier burden of proof. If a tidal wave hits the shore and I tell you I believe in earthquakes under the ocean floor, you won't look at me like I'm crazy. Neither of us may have seen the earthquake, but we've both just seen the wave.

———

Whether you're with me or not on the resurrection thing, consider what it would mean if it's true. This is where the surprise comes in with this last blessing. If evil is an unlimited asset, an endless energy with its own infinite life and resources, well then, evil can come after everyone and everything all the time. Persecution wouldn't really mean much because it would be indiscriminate. But evil is a limited resource. Why do I say that?

It comes from my reading of the crucifixion of Jesus. Evil exhausted its arsenal against him, and then, when evil had brought everything it had, when evil had mounted its greatest challenge to Love and put him in the grave, Love still had more to say. Resurrection is a story about the life of God, the Love of God, being inexhaustible, while evil runs its course. Resurrection is a story about the kingdom of heaven enduring.

This is why I believe evil is a limited resource.

I know. When the world breaks, it doesn't feel limited. It feels all-consuming. It seems like entropy has the final word. It feels like all our aspirations to build better worlds, all our bright moments that fade away, are just momentarily illusions, mirages in an infinite desert. But with every blessing, and with his own life, and especially in his death and resurrection, Jesus is saying that it's actually the other way around.

So even if you're not sure you believe me, even if this is hard to trust, just consider this logic for a moment. If, like evil, you're in a fight with limited resources, you don't expend those resources indiscriminately. You use them tactically. Surgically. With only so much ammo, you don't just pull the trigger and spray the field. You wait for your moment. You go after a high-value target.

And Jesus' last blessing is for people who find that they have become a target. That's what it means to be persecuted.

Do you see what that means?

Jesus began these blessings by speaking to us in what feels like our deepest powerlessness. He blessed us in our sadness. In our suffering.

He spoke to us in the broken-down conditions that emerge when the world breaks, and when it breaks us. But by the end, just a few blessings later, he's speaking to us with the assumption that we're going to need a blessing for the days when evil decides that we are the people who must be taken out. The sad sufferers have become the truly powerful ones. Not because we fought fire with fire. Not because we reacted violently. No—with the help of these surprising promises, we found our own tendencies to transmit our pain into the world being subverted. Instead of avoiding our suffering, we entered into it, not to wallow in it, not to identify with it, but to get to the bottom of it, to the Reality that was exposed by it.

And when we got to that Reality at the bedrock of things, we discovered that our emptiness was a gift made possible by permeable souls, and that we could be overwhelmed by the kingdom of God. We discovered that the glory we mourned for was never destroyed—it simply returned to God and perhaps came back to us in other forms. We discovered that everything we need is ours, whether we can demand it or not. We found ourselves filled from the feast-of-the-way-things-should-be even while we remain hungry for more.

We remembered the humanity we share with those in need of our mercy, a bond that runs deeper than the things that divide us. We discovered God hiding in the darkest shadows, even and especially in the faces of our enemies. We found a home in God, a sense of belonging that sustained us out beyond the circled wagons of our factions.

And because we did—because we were blessed in these strange, subversive ways—we became the people who put things back together. It turns out hope begins as a relationship with Reality, and it grows into the people we are becoming. Hope stretches itself out in the lives of people, not the optimists or the naïve, but the people who have met the Reality that Jesus calls the kingdom of heaven in their suffering, and who find themselves expanded and transformed.

———

Of course, that doesn't mean it will be easy. This isn't the kind of fake hope that tells you things are going to be fine. They're not. This world will continue to break, and it will continue to break us. It may even destroy us. The point isn't that things are going to be fine. The point is that there's something that happens on the other side of everything falling apart.

There's a lot of preaching out there that says that God will protect you. That because God loves you, because God claims you, because you're a member of God's family, somehow no evil can touch you. But if that's really true, then Jesus' own life wouldn't have ended the way it did.

There's a way of preaching the story of Jesus that says that Jesus died so we don't have to. But that's clearly not the witness of the New Testament. This story is saying that Jesus died to show us how to, and that after we're done dying, there will be another chapter in the story.

I've found those chapters written into my own life after those dark, dark days in the psych ward. I believe my friend Alex's story isn't over, that it's simply being lived in a new way, in a new realm, as he is held and healed in the love of God. I've lived those bright, beautiful chapters of resurrection now that the late-night calls from someone close to me aren't calls from crisis; they're conversations full of hope and growth and dreams.

———

So if you wake up one day and realize that you've been made a target, that evil in some form has made an agenda out of you, I hope you take it as a sign of promise. Something has happened in you and through you. A relationship with Reality has been forged. You're being transformed. You've probably stopped running from your suffering. You've also probably stopped waging war against evil with the same energies that fuel it. You're in the flow of a radical conversion in which suffering is turned into hope, and death becomes a resurrection.

11

A FINAL WORD

In the Jewish mystical tradition, one great rabbi taught his disciples that they should place the holy teachings on their heart. One day a student asked the rabbi why he always used the phrase "*on* your heart." The master replied, "Only God can put the teachings *in* your heart. Here, we recite and learn and put them on the heart hoping that someday when your heart breaks, they will fall in."*

This is how the mysteries come to us. Not as dictates from a distant God. Not as judgments that heap shame on us on our worst days. But as blessings that land lightly and gently, resting on the outer edge of the heart. When the world breaks, and when our hearts break with it, there's a chance that these blessings fall in.

When they do, they become guiding words, companions for the journey into the inner world of our suffering, assuring us that no amount of suffering can rob us of God. No defenses are required against the scariest experiences within. We don't have to wallow in our pain or identify with our losses. But we can be present with those things. We can be present with everything.

---

* I first read this Hasidic tale in an article from Parker Palmer at On Being's website: https://onbeing.org/blog/heartbreak-violence-and-hope-for-new-life/.

Our reactions can be dismantled. We can stop returning pain to the world for the pain it has caused us. We discover we have something better to give. The inward path that these blessings call us into leads us to an outer life only made possible by that inner expansion. It's not something we summon or create. It's something that flows through us when we allow ourselves to remain open.

Evil isn't afraid of the warriors for the cause. As long as we're still waging war, it doesn't matter what side of things we're on. We're still trying to put things together with the very same tools and energies that broke the world in the first place.

But when we consent to our own transformation, we become an entirely different kind of threat. It's not the warriors but the wounded healers who disrupt the evil and create new futures. When you find healing working in you and through you, evil will come for you. When it does, you'll know that your life has become a vessel for the kind of power that puts things back together. And while threats may come against you, you'll have nothing to fear.

———

Last summer I was in Northern Ireland and I stumbled into an unexpected opportunity to be with some of those wounded healers who are disrupting evil and creating new futures. The day was June 21, the longest day of the year, and a practice has emerged there of using that day to reflect on The Troubles and to consider the healing work that remains to be done. My friend Jonny was convening one of those Borderlands gatherings I mentioned in chapter 9 at the Pavilion Bar that night. We heard horrific stories of violence and terrorism and the misuse of religion and the tearing apart of families, and from the same people who told those stories, we also heard of healing and transformation. We heard stories of great hope from people who found that from the very places within where emptiness and ache were felt, there also emerged the unexpected possibility of new ways of relating. These people had been expanded by everything that had broken them.

Earlier that day, Jonny had asked if I might offer a final word at the end of the event. I struggled with the request. What kind of person opens their mouth when such sacred pain and such healing mysteries have been told by the people who have lived through them—especially when that person is an outsider to their stories, an American tourist who comes from a place where too many of us feel it's our place to show up in other places with naïve answers? I felt that my silence might be a good way to honor everything that would happen that night, and everything horrible and beautiful that happened in the history of that place.

But I didn't want to be rude. I did want to offer something to honor the people there, and being a preacher means I don't often have much to offer besides words. I trust Jonny, too, and figured he had a better sense than I of what would serve the moment.

Between lunch with Jonny when he asked me to share and

the event that evening where I would do it, I had a few hours to reflect. I scribbled random notes in a notebook, chasing ideas into dead ends, feeling more and more frustrated at what felt like the futility of my words in response to a world that can break in such heinous ways. Apparently, I was so troubled by the task that I was wearing the pain on my face, because at one point a stranger came up to me in the pub where I was working with my notepad and asked if I was all right. "You just look so sad," she said.

I was, in fact, very sad. I kept thinking about the different ways I had seen the world break. I thought about how we seem to repeat the same violence along the same lines, whether the fractures be personal or global. I felt the heaviness in my heart as memories filled my mind, knowing we have so much to weep for, and so much mending work to do.

But then I thought about these paradoxical words from Jesus, and the mysteries I had seen them point to again and again. I thought about the hope I had found in the psych ward where I could no longer pretend my soul hadn't been robbed by what happened. I thought about the heroes I had known in my city and in my church and in the West Bank and in Kenya and how their strength was almost always found on the other side of their breaking. I thought about the hillside church where Abuna Chacour had engraved the Beatitudes, where they met me in such a dark moment and led me into a kind of hope that has sustained me ever since.

So I brought a version of these blessings to the stage and set them loose, believing that they might continue to do what they have done for two thousand years, trusting that they would fall into the cracks of our broken hearts. In a room with all that pain and all that hope, this is roughly what I said:

When the world breaks,

And you find that you have been robbed in spirit
When you look to that place within where you would hope
   to find hope
And joy and power and peace
And instead find a poverty
May you know that you are in the terrain of heaven
Because the soul is not a closed system
We are conduits of God
And the open-heartedness that allowed you to be robbed as
   you suffered
is the very disposition that will allow you to be filled with
   the Divine.

When the world breaks,

And you suffer great loss
Whether it's the loss of hope
or the loss of a dream
or the loss of a beautiful arrangement
or the actual loss of someone you loved
May you mourn bravely
And in naming the void where the gift once stood

May you discover the eyes of your soul dilated
Your inner being flooded with light
For nothing good can ever be lost in God
And the glory we yearn for is still with us

When the world breaks,

And you find your strength bridled
Either by circumstance or systems
When you find yourself unable to take for yourself the
    things you need
May you trust that an open hand is all that's needed to
    receive
For you will inherit everything
As nothing Real was ever the possession of those who have
    bridled you in the first place

When the world breaks,

And you find yourself aching for things to be made right
Either within you or around you
Whether the fractures have happened in your life or have
    come against your life
May you trust the sacred pangs of hunger
May you know how holy your parched palate is
And rather than allowing your thirst to be slaked by false
    promises and faux justice
May your ache become a compass that leads you to a feast
    of peace

If you have been wronged and are finally given the rightful power of the victim to exact revenge,

> May you remember that you were forged from the same
>   moral fabric as the one who violated you
> And without creating a false equivalence between victims
>   and those who have perpetrated their suffering
> May we remember our own need for mercy

If you find your heart darkened by cynicism,

> May you see past the illusion that corruption is the final
>   word
> May your own shadows be the proving ground for a more
>   perceptive vision
> And may the eyes of your heart be enlightened,
> Giving you an uncommon capacity to see God,
> to see light,
> in even the darkest corners of our world

If you find yourself called out into the borderlands,

> Into the no-man's-land beyond your own faction
> Forsaking group belonging
> And if in those borderlands you find yourself desperately
>   alone
> Feared by your enemies and called a traitor by your own,
> May you discover that you have become a child of God,
>   claimed by the divine

May you discover a cosmic and irrevocable sense of
    belonging
as you walk the lonely path of peace

If you find yourself persecuted,

Made a target by the powers of disorder that are breaking
    the world
May you know that you have become a threat to the
    disorder
You have become a conduit of the divine
You have become an agent of love

So when the world breaks and it tries to break us,

May we trust that we, too, will be raised up.

Peace to you, friend.

ACKNOWLEDGMENTS

THANK YOU...

Carp, for the egregious sartorial consequences

Bible, for telling me to play it smart

Luke, for the thinly veiled threat of violence in every check-in on the manuscript

Wednesday Night Crew, for the sacred space at the table

Lighty, for the imagination

Chris, for keeping the door open to me all these years

Shauna, for introducing me to Chris

Beth A., for believing in this project

Chad, for late nights that don't go so late anymore

Manda, for challenging me to show up

Titus, for making it beautiful

Team Branning, for the exuberance

Kent and Becky, for showing me what faith in the unlearning is

Todd and Greg, for the 2010 trip and everything since

Aaron, for introducing me to Todd and Greg

Prashan and the whole Global Unites family, for the inspiration

Scott, for hearing something in my voice and telling me

Rick and Chelsea, for inviting me into that unlikely holy place in room 4106

Theo, for those Sunday afternoons in the kitchen

Cory and Caitlin, for reading those chapters in Montana

David and Jonny, for trusting an outsider

Beth C., for inviting me on to Team Alexander

South Bend City Church:

To our leaders on the board and staff team, for everything you've taught me

To our church family, for the ongoing experiment

Jeff, for showing me just how beautiful it is when things get put back together

Mom and Dad, for everything

ABOUT THE AUTHOR

Jason Adam Miller is the founder and lead pastor of South Bend City Church, an eclectic Christian community known for its thoughtful teaching, inclusive vision, and commitment to its city context. An advocate for artists and peacemakers, his work beyond South Bend focuses on cultural headwaters and conflict zones, where he serves an international constituency of leaders. He holds a master's degree in theology from the University of Notre Dame.